THE PSALMS

THE PSALMS

An Introduction

JAMES L. CRENSHAW

WILLIAM B. EERDMANS PUBLISHING COMPANY
GRAND RAPIDS, MICHIGAN / CAMBRIDGE, U.K.

© 2001 Wm. B. Eerdmans Publishing Co.

Wm. B. Eerdmans Publishing Co.
255 Jefferson Ave. S.E., Grand Rapids, Michigan 49503 /
P.O. Box 163, Cambridge CB3 9PU U.K.

Printed in the United States of America

05 04 03 02 01   7 6 5 4 3 2 1

Library of Congress Cataloging-in-Publication Data

Crenshaw, James L.
The Psalms: an introduction / James L. Crenshaw.
p.   cm.
Includes bibliographical references and index.
ISBN 0-8028-0854-9 (softcover: alk. paper)
1. Bible. O.T. Psalms — Introductions.

BS1430.52.C74 2001
223′.206 — dc21
                        00-049469

www.eerdmans.com

To
Connor, Clare, and Carolyn

Contents

Preface

For many years I have taught the book of Psalms to my students who were preparing for the ministry and for teaching in colleges, universities, seminaries, and divinity schools. In some ways those classes have brought me more satisfaction than many other seminars on various books of the Bible and topics related to advanced study of ancient Israelite literature. In the Psalms I have heard the voices of individuals who basked in the ecstasy of perceived divine presence and others who agonized over a sense of an absence. In these texts, too, I have discerned elegance both in word and in image, prayers rich in pathos, and hymns of elevated tone and subject. In them I have found kindred minds that have helped me frame my own thoughts about the mystery that enriches life and introduces pathos when least expected.

I wish to thank Allen Myers, Senior Editor at Eerdmans, for encouraging me to undertake the writing of this introduction and for patiently waiting when illness delayed its completion. That interim made it possible for me to read extensively in both primary and secondary literature. In accord with Allen's wishes, I have kept footnotes to a minimum, although that decision obscures my constant dialogue with the authors of many stimulating analyses of biblical psalms. From these authors I have learned much, but none of them has approached the book of Psalms in exactly the way I do. In short, I examine the nature of the several collections of psalms, look at comparable texts in the Bible and elsewhere, study different approaches to the Psalms, and take a close look at four psalms as an indication of the rich treasures awaiting diligent readers.

Two graduate students at Duke University kindly agreed to read the manuscript: Suzanne Henderson and Thea Portier-Young. I thank them for this generosity and for the privilege of teaching them. As always, I am indebted to Gail Chappell for transforming my handwritten text into a publishable form.

28 March 2000   JAMES L. CRENSHAW

Introduction

O ften called the hymnal of the Second Temple, the book of Psalms provides a window through which ancient Israel's response to God's presence, or absence, may be viewed. The one hundred and fifty psalms in the Masoretic Text give voice to a panoply of human emotions, sometimes sublime but at other times embarrassingly vengeful. The psalms arose in the experience of worship; in them both individual prayer and communal praise find expression, as do private reflection and learned instruction. Hardly a "little Bible," as Martin Luther claimed, the book of Psalms differs from the overwhelming majority of the other biblical writings that purport to declare divine revelation to Israel.

The human voice within the Psalms resonates with that of later worshippers, Christian and Jewish, who have found ways to recite the laments and hymns during worship. According to the Mishnah, Levites recited a psalm on each day of the week: Psalm 24 on Sunday, 48 on Monday, 82 on Tuesday, 94 on Wednesday, 81 on Thursday, 93 on Friday, and 92 on Saturday. *Ta'anit* 2:3 assigns Psalm 102 to days of fasting; Psalm 104 was used by Christians at the Feast of Pentecost. Psalm 136 is the great Hallel for Sabbath services, 113–118 the Egyptian Hallel. Seven psalms are known as penitential psalms (6, 32, 38, 51, 102, 130, and 143), and Psalm 79 is recited at the Western Wall in the Old City of Jerusalem on Friday evening, the ninth of Ab. The Septuagint and Talmud assign Psalm 93 to the eve of the Sabbath when God completed the creation of the world, and rabbinic tradition associates Psalm 95 with a New Year's festival.

1

Inspired by these biblical psalms, later worshippers wrote their own. One of these actually became canonical, the Septuagint having an additional one at the end, Psalm 151. All three major Greek manuscripts include it: Codex Sinaiticus, Alexandrinus (with the notation that the psalm is "outside the number"), and Vaticanus. An unknown Jewish author wrote eighteen psalms in the first century BCE, now called the Psalms of Solomon. The sectarians at Qumran, who occupied the area west of the Dead Sea from the middle of the second century BCE until the end of the first century CE, were particularly fond of psalms. Besides writing their own psalms of thanksgiving *(Hôdāyôt)* comprising about twenty-five psalms, they left behind an extensive cache of biblical psalms.[1] Nearby sites have also yielded Hebrew texts of Psalms (south of En Gedi, parts of 15-16; at Masada, parts of 81-85 and 150). In addition, four commentary texts have portions of psalms.

One of the oldest Hebrew manuscripts, the Aleppo Codex, lacks Ps 15:1–25:2; among Greek codices, Vaticanus does not have Ps 105:27–137:6 (added in the fifteenth century), and Alexandrinus lacks Ps 49:20–79:11. Sinaiticus preserves the complete book of Psalms. The numbering in the Masoretic Text (MT) differs from that in the Septuagint (LXX).

MT	LXX
1–8	1–8
9–10	9
11–113	10–112
114–115	113
116	114–115
117–146	116–145
147	146–147
148–150	148–150
	151

1. Fragments of 115 psalms have survived, along with a scroll, 11Q Ps^a, containing thirty-nine biblical psalms, 2 Sam 23:1-7, Sir 51:13-30, Psalms 151, 154, and 155. The actual sequence is: 101–103, 109, 118, 104, 147, 105, 146, 148, 121-32, 119, 135-36, 145, 154, "a Plea for Deliverance," 139, 137-138, Sir 51:13-30, "an Apostrophe to Zion," 93, 141, 133, 144, 155, 142-143, 149–150, "a Hymn to the Creator," 2 Sam 23:1-7, "a Prose Statement on David's Compositions," 140, 134, 151 A and B. Cave 11 also yielded another scroll with fragments of Psalms 141, 133, and 144. Yet another has noncanonical psalms but concludes with biblical Psalm 91.

The numbering in the Septuagint is supported by the fact that 9–10 were originally a single psalm, but the separation of Psalm 114 from 115 favors the numbering of the Masoretic Text. Both the Septuagint and the Masoretic Text divide a single psalm into 42–43. Confusion also results from the practice in the Masoretic Text of reckoning titles as the first verse. Some English versions follow this practice (NAB, JPS); others do not (e.g., RSV, KJV, NIV, TEV).

The early Christians sang hymns, although it is not clear whether these were taken from the Scriptures or composed by Christians (cf. Mark 14:26; Acts 4:24; 1 Cor 14:26; Eph 5:19; Col 3:16). It has been assumed that the New Testament cites Psalms from memory, but establishing actual quotations is difficult. Christian writers, for example, Clement of Rome (c. 90 CE), frequently cite Psalms (49 citations from 32 psalms in William Holladay's count),[2] as does the Didache, which dates from the end of the first century CE or the beginning of the second (Ps 37:11; 4:2; 118:26). In Justin's "Dialogue with Trypho" (mid-second century CE) there are forty-seven references to twenty-four psalms.

The name "Psalms" derives from the Greek *psalmoi,* songs of praise (Vaticanus has *psalmoi* as the title for Psalms; Sinaiticus has no title but concludes with "*psalmoi* of David"). "Psalter" comes from the title in Alexandrinus *(psalterion)* and indicates a musical instrument, presumably to accompany the singing of psalms. The Masoretic Text lacks a title, but that is typical for all the books in the Hebrew Bible; at the end of Psalm 72 it has "the prayers *(tepillôt)* of David have come to an end." Rabbinic literature prefers the terms *Tehillîm* and *Tillîm* (praises) to the Masoretic "prayers." Together these two, praise and prayer, describe the contents of the Psalter.

Like the Torah (Pentateuch), Psalms is divided into five books (1–41; 42–72; 73–89; 90–106; 107–150). Each of these books concludes with a doxology, a liturgical formula of praise to God (41:13; 72:19; 89:52; 106:48; 150). In Book I, closely associated with David by means of superscriptions, laments dominate. By Books IV and V praise comes to the forefront. The final five psalms are framed by the expression "Praise the Lord," which suggests that, in general, the book of Psalms

2. William L. Holladay, *The Psalms through Three Thousand Years: Prayerbook of a Cloud of Witnesses* (Minneapolis: Fortress, 1993), p. 162.

leads worshippers through grief to thanksgiving, from lament to praise.

Of the 150 psalms in the Masoretic Text, 116 have superscriptions. Virtually all of the psalms in Book I have superscriptions linking them to David. The exceptions are Psalms 1-2, 10, and 33, but the first two introduce the whole book of Psalms, whereas Psalms 10 and 33 are linked with the immediately preceding psalms. Book II duplicates two psalms in Book I (53 and 14; 70 and 40:14-18). An unusual feature of Books II-III is their preference for the divine name Elohim over Yahweh, but inconsistency abounds. Although Elohim occurs two hundred and forty-four times, Yahweh appears forty-four times in Psalms 42-83. In Book I Elohim is used only forty-nine times, and it occurs only seventy times in Psalms 84-150. With forty-four psalms, including the unique Psalm 119, Book V is the longest of the five. An alphabetic acrostic, Psalm 119 has eight lines beginning with the twenty-two letters of the Hebrew alphabet in sequence. Furthermore, each line has one of eight (possibly ten) synonyms for the law (except 90, which has a ninth synonym, and 122). Less complex acrostics include Psalms 25, 34, 111, 112, and 145 (cf. the irregular pattern in Psalms 9-10, where nearly every second verse begins with a letter of the alphabet in sequence).

The titles of individual psalms range from a single word (in Psalm 98, *mizmôr*, "a psalm") to extensive comment (18, "To the choirmaster. A Psalm of David the servant of the Lord, who addressed the words of this song to the Lord on the day when the Lord delivered him from the hand of all his enemies, and from the hand of Saul. He said."). Only thirty-four psalms lack titles (I, 1-2, 10, and 33; II, 43 and 71; IV, 91, 93, 94-97, 99, and 104-106; V, 107, 111-119, 135-137, and 146-150). Perhaps the invitation to praise the Lord functioned as a substitute for a title in Psalms 111-113, 117, 135, and 146-150. Twelve titles recall particular events in David's life (3, 7, 18, 51, 52, 54, 56-57, 59-60, 63, and 142). Another fifty-five have a specific liturgical instruction, "to the leader," while others refer to musical instruments and to things that scholars have not been able to identify. Still others record genre designations such as prayer, praise, song, *maskîl, miktām,* and *šiggāyôn.*[3] Considerably more variation in titles from the Masoretic Text exists in

---

3. On technical terms in the superscriptions, see Sigmund Mowinckel, *The Psalms in Israel's Worship* (Nashville: Abingdon, 1962), pp. 207-17.

Books IV and V in the Qumran manuscripts. The term *mizmôr* is found fifty-seven times, and *selāh*, which seems to indicate a break or pause, occurs in the body of some psalms (it also appears in psalms outside the book of Psalms, e.g., in Hab 3:3, 9, and 13; in Hab 3:19 one also finds "To the choirmaster: with stringed instruments").

The tendency during the postexilic period to attribute sacred writings to revered leaders — the Pentateuch to Moses, the Wisdom Literature to Solomon, prophetic texts like Isaiah 40–66 to Isaiah — led to an identification of David as the author of numerous psalms. The attribution of psalms to him in 2 Sam 1:19-27 and 22:2-51 (which also appears as Psalm 18), together with the tradition that he was a musician (1 Sam 18:10; Amos 6:5), encouraged this trend. The Septuagint carries it even beyond the point reached by the Masoretic Text, increasing the number of psalms attributed to David from seventy-three to eighty-five. Although the Hebrew *ledāwid* (pertaining to David) does not necessarily mean Davidic authorship, its intent seems to have been that in many instances. It could also suggest that the particular psalm was written for a collection honoring David. The Qumran sectarians left no doubt about their view; a note states that David composed 3,600 psalms and 446 songs, plus four for the stricken, totaling 4,050 (cf. 1 Kings 4:32 [MT 5:12] for a similar comment about Solomon's literary productivity — 3,000 proverbs, 1,005 songs).

Not every psalm is credited to David, or even associated with him in some manner. Other persons honored in this way include Jeduthun (39, 62, and 77), Heman (88), Solomon (72, 127), Moses (90), Ethan (89), and two musical guilds, the Korahites (42, 44–49, 84–85, and 87–88) and the Asaphites (50, and 70–83). The family of Asaph is said to have been active as late as the Josianic reforms (621 BCE) and during the time of Ezra and Nehemiah nearly two centuries later.

When were the psalms written? Certain similarities with Canaanite texts from Ugarit have suggested an early date for Psalms 29, 82, and 19:2-7, but late texts (cf. Daniel) also show affinities with this literature. Plausible connections with David make Psalms 2, 110, and 18 viable candidates for the tenth century, or at the very least they imply a date during the monarchy. Several psalms reflect interests in the North, leading some critics to think they derive from the northern kingdom prior to its defeat by Assyrian soldiers in 722 BCE. Other psalms seem to assume the existence of a monarchy: for example, Psalms 2, 18, 20–21,

45, 72, 89, 101, 110, 132, and 144. Linguistic features point to a postexilic date for Psalms 103, 117, 119, 124–125, and 145. Content alone places Psalm 137 in postexilic times ("By the waters of Babylon, there we sat down and wept when we remembered Zion"). Every attempt to date psalms encounters enormous difficulty, for their content is altogether indifferent to historical events except those serving paradigmatically (e.g., the exodus from Egypt).

The Early Church understood the psalms as personal expressions of worship in definite historical contexts. That approach prevailed until the nineteenth century, when critical scholars began to emphasize the genres of individual psalms and to stress their congregational origin. The ground-breaking work of Hermann Gunkel elevated form criticism to pride of place,[4] and this approach has continued to the present. Essentially, it distinguishes the following literary types: lament (both individual and communal), thanksgiving hymn (individual and communal), royal enthronement psalms, wisdom and torah psalms, entrance liturgies, prophetic exhortation, and mixed forms. Laments routinely include an opening address, description of trouble, petition, expression of confidence, and a vow. Thanksgiving songs include praise, description of past trouble, testimony, and exhortation. Naturally, individual psalms vary the elements, and it is often impossible to distinguish between a lament and a song of thanksgiving that presupposes the situation described in laments, whereas the expression of confidence resembles thanksgiving. Moreover, some designations of genre are based on content; that is true of royal psalms, songs of Zion, and wisdom and torah psalms.

Form critics sought to illuminate the social setting of individual psalms. Accordingly, they posited special festivals (Sigmund Mowinckel: an enthronement festival; Hans-Joachim Kraus: a royal Zion festival; Artur Weiser: a covenant renewal ceremony; Erhard Gerstenberger: liturgical sermons).[5] The Akitu, or New Year's Festival, in ancient Babylonia was often assumed to have a corollary in Judah, with annual coronation of the Davidic king. For this occasion royal psalms such as 2, 18, 20, 21, 72, 89, 101, 110, 132 and 144 are thought to have

---

4. Hermann Gunkel, *An Introduction to the Psalms* (Macon, Ga.: Mercer University Press, 1998 [*Einleitung in die Psalmen*, 1933]).

5. No single solution to the cultic context for the Psalms has yet emerged.

been used. Entrance liturgies would have served to prepare worshippers before they entered the holy temple (15 and 24). A royal wedding gave rise to Psalm 45; didactic or learned instruction produced many psalms (e.g., 19, 119, 78, 89); and prophetic exhortation yielded Psalms 50, 81, and 95. Songs of Zion give voice to the people's fondness for Jerusalem as the divine dwelling place (46, 48, 76, 84, 87, and 122). Another group of psalms is presumed to have been sung as pilgrims made their way to Jerusalem (120–134) or as priests ascended the steps within the temple.

Some psalms seem to relate to individuals during times of extraordinary suffering brought on by illness, attack by foreign armies, slander, magical practices, and the like. Others give voice to private joy and public expressions of honor. Individuals express their deepest emotions in prayer: sometimes they are in near despair, and at other times they are barely able to contain their jubilation. Locating precise settings for all of these has resulted in little more than vague generalities.

For this and other reasons, interpreters have begun to emphasize the rhetoric of psalms, their persuasive use of language. Advances in the understanding of poetry have isolated numerous features of the psalms. The balancing of one colon with another is achieved through various means, but prominence is usually given to chiasm (the forming of an X by structuring a poem as follows: ABB′A′). Repetition takes place in a number of ways. James Limburg lists the following: question and answer; statement and quotation; a "better than" expression; variation of theme (A) and repeated refrain (B); abstract and concrete; whole and synecdoche (a figure of speech in which a more inclusive term is used for a less inclusive term or vice versa); two terms as a merismus (expressing wholeness, e.g., heaven and earth, great and small); and simile and reality.[6]

In some circles, rhetorical criticism has virtually superseded form criticism, resulting in special emphasis on repetition, chiasm, inclusions, structure, and figurative language. Whether many of the features isolated in this manner result from authorial intention or not has yet to be established. That judgment applies particularly to analysis of structure, often the result of highly subjective reading, and to inclusions, which may be accidental, given the repetitive demands of Hebrew poetry and the limited vocabulary available to composers.

6. James Limburg, "Psalms, Book of," in *ABD*, vol V (Garden City, N.Y.: Doubleday, 1992), pp. 522-36.

Not every interpreter focuses on the structure of a single psalm. Some critics examine the macrostructure, hoping to explain the overall shaping of the book of Psalms. Gerald Wilson has argued that the complete collection of five books is arranged to show how the covenant between God and David as king became bankrupt and the kingship of Yahweh took its place.[7] Wilson thinks the presence of royal psalms at the beginning of Book I (2) and at the conclusion of Books II and III (72 and 89) documents a move from an intimate relationship between the king and God and its reinforcement through ritualistic ceremony to a rehearsal of a wrenching rejection of the covenant with David. The purpose of these psalms (specifically 2, 72, and 89) was to document the failure of the Davidic covenant. The initial psalm (1) emphasizes the individual relationship with God, whereas Psalm 2 stresses the corporate dimension. Books IV and V move in another direction entirely, demonstrating that Israel's true home is God, the only dependable ruler. The heart of the Psalter, in this reading, resides in Book IV. This theological center clarifies the real nature of monarchy, a theocracy. Book V transfers to the people the former royal claims associated with David. The result is a resounding triumph of eschatological praise. The Psalter defines happiness (cf. 1:1, "Happy is the one who . . .") in quite concrete ways, but at the heart of the definition is the concept of trust and refuge.

Other interpreters understand the overall structure of Psalms differently. Two of these views merit attention here: a movement from lament to praise,[8] and an increasingly liturgical movement.[9] The first of these attributes significance to the early positioning of laments, for praise cannot achieve its goal until religious people have wrestled with their own doubts and emerged from them in the way described so effectively in Psalm 73. The second approach acknowledges that the early laments emphasize David's humanity and consequently the demise of his dynasty, but it recognizes the growing importance of liturgical guilds

---

7. Gerald Wilson, *The Editing of the Hebrew Psalter,* SBLDS 76 (Chico, Calif.: Scholars Press, 1985).

8. The preponderance of laments in the early collection of "Davidic psalms" and the grouping of psalms of praise at the end of the Psalter make this hypothesis rather obvious. The issue is complicated by the occurrence of laments after praise has become common.

9. Carroll Stuhlmueller, "Psalms," in *Harper's Bible Commentary* (San Francisco: Harper and Row, 1988), p. 433.

(Book III) and cultic events (pilgrimages and festivals [Book V, 120–134 for pilgrimages, 113–118 for three major festivals]). Notably, the opening word in 1:1, *'ašrē* (happy), is more secular than *bārûk* (blessed). The closing exhortation, "Praise the Lord," belongs to sacred discourse. This final psalm, 150, has ten *hallelûjāhs* (or *hallelûhûs*) or thirteen if one counts the conclusion in verse 6 and the opening and closing ones. Carroll Stuhlmueller thinks these numbers correspond to the Decalogue and the thirteen attributes of Yahweh revealed to Moses in Exod 34:6-7, or the thirteen times God spoke in Genesis 1.[10]

The rich theological dimension of the Psalter continues to press itself on Jews and Christians. The metaphors for God serve in prayer and worship to convey deep feelings of trust and abandonment. The psalmists praise God as king, judge, shepherd, rock, portion, light, warrior, father, and farmer. They describe the people in a role of dependency as vine, tree, sheep, quiver, and the like. They distinguish between the righteous and wicked, promising life in its fullness to the former and destruction to the latter. Such evil practitioners are likened to grass, chaff, and dust; in the language of Psalm 1, their roots lack adequate water. Sinners did prosper, much to the chagrin of psalmists, but their prosperity was believed to be short-lived. A few psalmists probe deeply into traditional belief, in one instance breaking new ground and approaching, if not actually attaining, belief in life beyond the grave (73).

The book of Psalms has provided a reservoir from which poets have drawn in composing hymns, a practice already engaged in by composers of some psalms who produced mosaics of biblical passages (cf. 96–97, 119, 135). Individual psalms have contributed both language and sentiment for meditating about God and the law, and one psalm, the twenty-third, has become a virtual icon in the United States, as William Holladay has shown.[11] Another psalm, 46, is the basis for Martin Luther's hymn, "Ein' Feste Burg." The psalms may be ancient Israel's response to God's self-manifestation, but to many modern worshippers they represent authentic worship. They plumb the depths of despair through which many pass at one time or another, and they soar to lofty heights of adoration, to which good people aspire. In short, from these majestic psalms one learns how to pray.

---

10. Stuhlmueller, "Psalms," p. 433.
11. Holladay, *The Psalms through Three Thousand Years*, pp. 359-71.

FURTHER READING

Barth, Christoph. *Introduction to the Psalms.* New York: Scribner's, 1966.

Gerstenberger, Erhard. *Psalms. Part I, with an Introduction to Cultic Poetry.* FOTL 14. Grand Rapids: Eerdmans, 1988.

Gunkel, Hermann. *The Psalms: A Form-Critical Introduction.* Philadelphia: Fortress, 1967.

Holladay, William L. *The Psalms through Three Thousand Years: Prayerbook of a Cloud of Witnesses.* Minneapolis: Fortress, 1993.

Limburg, James. "Psalms, Book of." In *Anchor Bible Dictionary,* vol V, pp. 522-36. Garden City, N.Y.: Doubleday, 1992.

McCann, J. Clinton, Jr. "Psalms." In *New Interpreter's Bible,* vol IV, pp. 641-1280. Nashville: Abingdon, 1996.

Miller, Patrick D. *Interpreting the Psalms.* Philadelphia: Fortress, 1986.

Seybold, Klaus. *Introducing the Psalms.* Edinburgh: T & T Clark, 1990.

Stuhlmueller, Carroll. "Psalms." In *Harper's Bible Commentary,* pp. 433-95. San Francisco: Harper and Row, 1988.

PART I

ORIGINS

✦ CHAPTER ONE ✦

The Individual Collections

Hymns and Laments in Ancient Egypt and Mesopotamia

During good times peoples of the ancient Near East raised their voices in praise of their gods, thanking them for providential care and promising loyalty in thought and deed. Among other things, the god being addressed is credited with creating everything that exists and providing sustenance for all creatures; recognized as sole deity, unique among the pantheon of gods; extolled as powerful conqueror of all foes, including the dragon chaos; lauded as champion of the poor and defenseless; celebrated as healer and judge; viewed as shepherd, father, and king; characterized as merciful and forgiving; and recognized as mysterious and invisible yet near enough to answer prayer.

A few of these hymns focus entirely on the well-being of a king, whose health and prosperity are closely tied up with that of his subjects. Some of these hymns are occasioned by official events such as the king's enthronement, while others provide legitimating credentials and offer religious sanction for his actions. The language of election while in the womb, divine protection, and extraordinary attributes functions as society's means of assuring itself that order will prevail and that loyalty will be rewarded.

During periods of adversity the people cried out in pain, informing the gods of their suffering and imploring them to intervene on their behalf. These prayers normally took the form of laments, sometimes na-

13

tional and at other times personal. These lamentations cover far-reaching calamities such as the burning of the city Ur, with which Abraham is associated in biblical tradition, and private misery of various kinds. The question "How long?" occurs with relentless abandon, as if to underline the speaker's inability to comprehend any legitimate reason for the distress. Protests of innocence intermingle with admission of wrongdoing, but both of these pale in comparison with the emphasis on the incomprehensibility of the deity's actions. Even that acknowledgment of human finitude is overshadowed by the description of misery, for which no relief is in sight. Nevertheless, the liturgical use of these texts suggests that those persons who utter them do so in expectation of successfully influencing the deity being addressed.

The Book of Psalms

The actual authors of the psalms in the Bible are unknown, although tradition has provided several names ranging from Moses to little-known temple singers centuries later. King David either has been credited with the authorship of the majority of individual psalms or has been associated with them in some way. Most of them were probably written anonymously, like the preponderance of literature in the ancient world. The compositions eventually gained acceptance as expressions of communal concerns and were used in the cult of the temple and in synagogues.

Unlike much biblical literature, these psalms originated from below. They constitute human praise and requests for help, in short, prayers. The only internal attempt to describe the psalms notes that "The prayers of David, son of Jesse, have ended" (Ps 72:20); this observation applies only to the first two divisions (3–41, 42–72). The books of Proverbs, Job, and Ecclesiastes in the Hebrew Bible join them in expressing human speech. Most other books purport to present God's revelation to humanity or give an account of divine action as understood by the authors. Exceptions do occur: for example, Song of Songs, the book of Esther, and in a different way the beautiful book of Ruth.

Brief superscriptions offer the oldest interpretive clue for the psalms. Their authenticity cannot be proven, but they provide a convenient way of introducing the various themes of the prayers. Only twenty-four psalms lack an inscription, the remaining one hundred and twenty-six being associated with David (in all, seventy-three psalms), Solomon (72), Moses (90), or musical guilds (Asaph, Korah, and Ethan). Musical notations appear as headings of a host of psalms: *mizmôr* (fifty-seven times), *lamnaṣṣēaḥ* (fifty-five times), and *šîr* (thirty times). The precise meaning of these and other notations has not survived, although they probably offered clues about melodies and identified specific types of songs. The inscription *šîr hamma'ălôt* (Song of the Ascents, with the following variations: Song for the Ascents in 121; Song of the Ascents for David in 122, 124, 131, 133; Song of the Ascents for Solomon in 127) is the only one that occurs in an integral unit, fifteen consecutive psalms. All other inscriptions are scattered throughout the Psalter.

Psalms Attributed to David

Seventy-three psalms, nearly half of the total in the Bible, bear a superscription in which the name David appears. Virtually all the psalms in Book I fall into this group, as do eighteen psalms from Book II. The third and fourth books have only one and two respectively, whereas Book V has fifteen superscriptions referring to David. The Septuagint extends the total number to eighty-five. Many of these superscriptions take the form of the preposition *lāmed* attached to the name David. The resulting linguistic form has several meanings: to or for David, concerning David, or by David. It does not necessarily suggest Davidic authorship, although later interpreters may have read the expression this way.

Thirteen of the seventy-three superscriptions mention specific incidents in David's life as reported in 1 and 2 Samuel. Rather than examining all the psalms attributed to David, we shall take a quick look at these thirteen (3, 7, 18, 34, 51–52, 54, 56–57, 59–60, 63, 142). The dominant theme in this small group, lament, gives these psalms a sense of sameness. A cry for help coupled with deep trust in the one to whom the prayer is addressed runs throughout both collections. Occasionally, the complaint recedes entirely and an expression of confidence stands alone.

The Sixty-third Psalm best exemplifies this boundless optimism. It voices the intensity of emotional intimacy between the psalmist and God, a love that rivals that of a man and a woman. Physical desire for water by a parched land provides the simile for the depth of intimacy enjoyed here. Indeed, the psalmist even considers God's love the highest good, better than life itself, and thinks such ardor will endure until his dying moment. In the shadow of divine wings the poet finds rest; the single comment about danger takes the form of confidence that foes will die. Here we encounter the only reference to a king in these psalms. David's sojourn in the wilderness of Judah seems an appropriate setting for this beautiful psalm.

Psalm 34, an acrostic with one Hebrew letter missing *(waw)* and with two letters transposed *(ayin* and *pe),* voices thanks for victory and Yahweh's continued protection. The heavy manner in which the psalmist draws attention to the educative task sets this psalm apart, especially the appeal to children, with promise of instruction in religion, which entails integrity and turning away from evil. Yahweh's fondness for the brokenhearted gives voice to a comforting assurance that not one bone of a just person will be broken. Yahweh's protection of David when he feigned madness before Abimelech was thought to be an appropriate occasion for this psalm. According to 1 Sam 21:13-16, David used this ploy in the presence of Achish, not Abimelech.

One psalm in this group is a duplicate of the royal thanksgiving for victory attributed to David in 1 Samuel 22. The original superscription recurs in the Psalter, with the addition of the honorific "the servant of the Lord" after David's name. We shall treat this psalm in the section on biblical hymns outside the Psalter.

The majority of laments give the impression of having been composed for use by a single individual, but exceptions such as Psalm 60 lend a communal dimension to the voice of distress. Here the superscription refers to traditional lore that David fought against Aram-Naharaim and Aram-Zobah and that Joab slew 12,000 Edomites in the Valley of Salt. Eschatological language of judgment occurs in this psalm, especially the cup of wine that God forces the condemned to drink and the splitting of the earth. Similarly, the psalm's primary interest, the allocation of land to the just, belongs to scenes of a final judgment. Two images, the casting of a sandal over an area and the description of Edom as a washbowl, emphasize God's ownership. The tone of the psalm derives from its initial sense of divine rejection and the agonizing question, "Do you no longer march with our armies?" The twofold appeal for help further emphasizes the despairing attitude before the deity who owns the territories that have fallen out of the control of God's people.

Psalm 52 goes on the attack against arrogant slanderers. The psalmist believes that God will uproot such evildoers while causing the poet to take root in God's house like an olive tree. The application to an event in David's life seems forced, for the complaint of the psalm concerns slander rather than exposure of someone's hiding place, in this instance David's residence with Ahimelech (1 Sam 21:2-10). Psalm 54 is connected with similar disclosure, this time by Ziphites who told Saul that David was hiding in their midst (1 Sam 23:19). This psalm implores the deity for help and promises generous gifts in return.

Seldom does a psalmist insist on innocence, but Psalm 7 rules out personal iniquity as a basis for discomfiture. The psalmist believes so strongly in this claim that he is willing to risk the future on it: "If I am guilty, let my enemy prevail." The justice of Yahweh is taken for granted here, but that does not rule out an appeal for convincing demonstration that evil returns to its perpetrator and that sinners conceive and give birth to nothing of consequence. How this affirmation of divine justice pertains to David's relationship with Cush the Benjaminite is not clear. Psalm 3, which announces that Yahweh heard the psalmist's cry and became a shield against many foes, is a much clearer instance of a fit between its content and the superscription. The association of this psalm with the occasion of Absalom's rebellion does not require much imagination, although the threefold use of the Hebrew term *selāh* points to liturgical use and thus to a general rather than specific occasion.

Psalm 51, one of seven penitential psalms according to the later Church, has been linked to David's repentance over his adulterous affair with Bathsheba and his command that Joab arrange for the death of her husband Uriah the Hittite. At least one verse (v. 20) rules out Davidic authorship, for its reference to the broken walls of Jerusalem demands a date after 587 BCE. Furthermore, the psalmist's restriction of sins to the vertical dimension hardly applies to David, who wronged both God and at least two people. These observations do nothing to detract from the enormous spiritual power of the confession. The psalmist recognizes sin as the human condition and pleads for cleansing that will make sounds of praise ring forth. Yahweh's fondness of a contrite spirit receives special mention here, together with the need for divine instruction. The prerequisite for a proper cult, a pure heart, also surfaces in this psalm.

Requests for Yahweh's mercy characterize Psalms 56 and 57. The first of these, linked with David when Philistines seized him at Gath (1 Sam 21:10-15), admits that enemies surround the poet but expresses complete trust in divine protection. Confident that mere flesh cannot prevail against God's chosen, the psalmist believes that his tears are stored in a vial, indeed that his name is recorded in a heavenly scroll. The twofold reference to mere flesh varies the language, using *bāśār* in the first instance and *ʾādām* in the second. Psalm 57 describes the speaker's plight in graphic detail, but the problem appears to be slander, not danger from lions. The psalmist personifies the lyre and harp, urging them to awake (cf. 108:3), and expresses trust in God Most High, whose love and faithfulness reach the heavens. Nevertheless, a twofold refrain in verses 6 and 12 pleads with God to appear. The superscription refers to David's flight from Saul into a cave.

Psalm 142 also mentions David's attempt to hide in a cave. The psalmist has a keen sense of entrapment with no escape in sight, but this situation only reinforces a conviction of divine support. Boldly the poet begs for rescue from prison. Psalm 59 depicts an innocent individual who has been ambushed by powerful enemies. The reference to nations fits badly with the superscription, which mentions Saul's emissaries who are searching for David. The arrogance of the peoples who question God's ability to hear anything provokes laughter above and an appeal from below for a divine show of force on Jacob's behalf. A refrain in verses 7 and 15 emphasizes the recurrence of the threat.

The Songs of Ascents (120-134)

This group of Ascent psalms seems to have been associated with pilgrimages to Jerusalem, although only Psalm 122 actually alludes to a journey with Zion as its goal. Curiously, the language of at least three other psalms connects them with sacred processions into the holy city (24, 43, 84). The expression *maʿălôt* (ascending) has given rise to different theories about its connotation.[1] Three views grow out of the sense of physical ascent, while others stress the symbolic use of the word.

1. Daniel Grossberg, *Centripetal and Centrifugal Structures in Biblical Poetry*, SBLMS 39 (Atlanta: Scholars Press, 1989).

Return from Exile

On the basis of Ezra 7:9, where *hamma'ălâ* occurs with reference to Judean exiles returning to Jerusalem from Babylon, some interpreters have understood the inscription to Psalms 120–134 as a reference to these pilgrims. This explanation runs into difficulty, for Psalms 122 and 134 imply that a temple was standing at the time. That was not true in 539 BCE. Indeed, the dedication of the second temple did not take place until 516, largely the result of activity spurred on by the prophets Haggai and Zechariah.

Annual Pilgrimages

Others understand the inscription in light of the three annual pilgrimages to Jerusalem mandated in Deut 16:16 and Exod 23:13-17; 34:18-23. Nowhere, however, does the word *ma'ălôt* appear in connection with these three festivals (Passover, Weeks, and Sukkot or Booths).

Climbing the Steps inside the Temple

Biblical reference to Levites ascending steps within the temple (Exod 20:26 and 1 Kings 10:19-20) generated speculation in the Mishnah that *ma'ălôt* refers to priestly activity. In *Mid.* 2:5 one reads: "Fifteen steps led up from within it [Court of the Women] to the Court of the Israelites, corresponding to the fifteen Songs of Ascents in the Psalms, and upon them the Levites used to sing. . . ." Another text, *Sukk.* 5:4, remarks that numerous Levites played several musical instruments on the fifteen steps leading from the Court of the Israelites, corresponding to the fifteen Songs of Ascents. The presence of four words from the levitical blessing in Num 6:24-26 (bless, protect, be gracious to, peace) has led one scholar to see the rationale for the inscription in the Levites' pronunciation of this blessing on the steps of the temple.

With Elevated Voice

On the basis of 2 Chron 20:19, where Levites are said to have praised Yahweh with a loud, raised voice, some critics have understood the inscription in the sense of a high pitch. This view had the endorsement of the eminent Jewish interpreter Saadiah Gaon (882-942), according to an observation by David Kimhe (1160-1235) in his commentary on Psalms.

A Poetic Device: Stairstep Structure

A notable feature of many of these psalms is their ascending structure, the frequent use of incremental parallelism. In the first colon the poet introduces an image that leads on to its completion in the second colon, as in Ps 121:2 ("My help comes from Yahweh, the maker of heaven and earth"). Words in one verse are repeated in later verses as well. This stylistic device of incrementalism occurs frequently in psalms outside the unit under discussion and cannot supply the key to the meaning of the inscription.

Rising from Adversity

Jeremiah's counsel to sing and praise Yahweh for delivering the poor from evildoers (Jer 20:13) has been understood as a key to the noun *šîr* in the inscriptions. In this view, the songs are expressions of gratitude for deliverances from threatening circumstances. Of the fifteen psalms, however, only Psalms 120 and 124 actually accord with such a reading.

Advance in Spiritual Life

The sublimity of the religious sentiments in some of these psalms, especially 121; 123:1-3; and 131, has led scholars to view the group as an expression of spiritual growth. The Songs of Ascents do not, however, have a monopoly on such elevated feelings, nor do they sustain this lofty spirituality (cf. 129).

What can be said, then, about the meaning of the inscription? Because several of the psalms are appropriate for pilgrims (122) and their enthusiasm for Zion (125, 126-129, 132-134), some association with pilgrims seems justified, especially if one broadens the interpretation to include progress in spiritual growth. Some of the psalms may originally have been sung by pilgrims, and others were probably added to give the collection abiding value for persons residing in Jerusalem and its immediate environs. The lasting impression that songs of rejoicing by individuals journeying to Jerusalem made on the prophet Isaiah (30:29) strengthens this interpretation.

As a group, these psalms stand out for reasons other than their inscriptions. With only eighteen verses, Psalm 132 is the longest of the group; all the others have fewer than nine verses, and Psalms 131, 133, and 134 have only three verses each. Apart from Psalm 117, the shortest psalm in the Bible is 134. (By contrast, the longest psalm, 119, with 176 verses, stands just before the Song of Ascents.) Moreover, these psalms abound in rare words and use others proportionately more than anywhere else.[2]

This collection of 101 verses employs rich images for the intimacy enjoyed between worshippers and Yahweh. The notion of watching over someone (*šmr*, six times in vv. 3-8) pervades Psalm 121, echoing numerous references to divine protection. In Psalm 123, dependence on Yahweh's favor is graphically likened to male and female slaves looking to their masters for signs of kindness. The hills surrounding Zion evoke the comforting thought of encompassing divine arms (125:2). Weeping transformed into shouts of joy over bountiful crops signals restored fortunes in Psalm 126:5-6. Children resemble arrows in a quiver (127:3-5), and speech as arrows with flaming tips echoes the devastating force of slander (120:2, 4). Persons who fear Yahweh can count on domestic tranquility, with wives like vines and children resembling olive trees (128:1-4). In company with Job of old, they will see their grandchildren (128:6). The devout soul waits for Yahweh as eagerly as a sentinel anticipates dawn's light (130:5-6). A humble worshipper calms an

---

2. The particle *hinnēh* (seven times, over 25% of its uses in Psalms), *kēn* (25%), *rabbat* (four of its seven uses in the Masoretic Text), *'im lō'* (three times), and *sĕ-* (nine), *šām* with the meaning Jerusalem (122:4, 5; 132:17; 133:3). Grossberg, *Centripetal and Centrifugal Structures in Biblical Poetry*, pp. 49-50.

anxious mind just as mothers quiet their weaned children (131). Unity is like precious ointment running down Aaron's beard and the collar of his robe (133).

Repeated expressions also highlight this unit. The divine epithet, "maker of heaven and earth," occurs three times (121:2; 124:8; 134:3), and the adverbial expression denoting endurance, "now and for a long time," appears an equal number of times (121:8; 125:2; 131:3). In Psalm 121 the close relationship with Yahweh is reinforced by pronominal suffixes (*kā*, ten times) and frequent uses of the divine name written as YHWH without vowels and known to scholars as the Tetragrammaton (four times, six more times implicitly). Puns on the name *šālēm* (peace) abound in Ps 122:6-7, and the inclusio "house of Yahweh" marks verses 1 and 9. A hint in Ps 124:1 and 129:1 ("Let Israel say . . .") suggests antiphonal chant, the voice of the people urged on by the poet. Reasoned argument, brought to a temporary conclusion only to be resumed promptly, marks Ps 124:1-5. An echo of the danger inherent to unpunished evil, the seducing of good people to abandon the way of integrity, connects Psalm 125 to the problem envisioned in the earlier Psalm 73. The vanity of human endeavor, apart from divine surveillance and active support, comes to expression in Ps 127:1-2.

The association of Psalm 127 with the name Solomon in the inscription was an extrapolation from the topic of verse 1, building a house. The reference to Yahweh's guarding the city suggested to someone Solomon's construction of the temple over which Yahweh stood guard. The reason for adding the name David to the inscription of four psalms of this group is less obvious, apart from the recognizable tendency to connect as many psalms as possible to him. Notably, the psalm that replaces the absolute divine promise to David with a conditional sentence ("If your sons keep my covenant, and the laws that I teach them, their sons will successively occupy your throne forever," 132:12) does not mention him in the inscription.

Do the fifteen psalms show any movement that might explain their present order? Progress from a cry of distress to complete confidence has been detected, with Jerusalem occupying a central role in the threefold process of spiritual maturation (120–122, 123–128, 129–134). The second psalm in the series already casts suspicion on such an analysis, for it breathes an atmosphere of trust in Yahweh's protection.

The Psalms of Asaph

Twelve psalms bear an inscription relating them to Asaph, about whom little is known.[3] Of these, two substitute *maskîl* for *mizmôr* (74 and 78); the variations with *mizmôr* seem to indicate melodies and proprietorship. With a single exception (50), these psalms (73–83) constitute a discrete unit within the larger book. They exhibit remarkable cohesion with respect to theme. The initial psalm asserts that the heavens proclaim divine justice; for the most part, the other eleven psalms reflect on the accuracy of this claim in light of evidence to the contrary, particularly Jerusalem's ruined state and the prosperity of the wicked. They move from the promise of Yahweh's coming that corrects previous silence (50:3) and the justification of speech (50:21), through the announcement that the earth has been reduced to silence (76:9), to a plea for the fulfillment of the promise that God will not remain silent (83:2).

The emphasis on theodicy[4] gives rise to an astonishing elevation of that issue to a divine council, where God (*'elōhîm*) sits in judgment over the other deities and condemns them for failing to protect the poor and powerless members of society (82). The abdication of responsibility for promoting the welfare of marginalized citizens costs them their lives. For behaving like humankind, these heavenly beings, offspring of the Most High, will suffer the fate of mortals. Only thus will earth's shaky foundations return to normal, with the restoration of order as its basis. Curiously, the divine name Yahweh is missing where one most expects a declaration of exclusive rule by the Lord of the covenant. Does the final appeal to arise and judge earth's inhabitants conceal a subtle indictment of Yahweh?

If the universe in some fashion declares divine justice, and if God holds the lesser heavenly beings to this exemplary ideal, why does Yahweh not take a bold stand against vicious soldiers who burned Jeru-

---

3. Michael D. Goulder, *The Psalms of Asaph and the Pentateuch,* JSOTSS 233 (Sheffield: Sheffield Academic Press, 1996), pp. 312-27, discusses the evidence.

4. On theodicy, see James L. Crenshaw, *Urgent Advice and Probing Questions: Collected Writings on Old Testament Wisdom* (Macon, Ga.: Mercer University Press, 1995), pp. 141-221, and "The Sojourner Has Come to Play the Judge: Theodicy on Trial," in *God in the Fray: A Tribute to Walter Brueggemann,* ed. Tod Linafelt and Timothy K. Beal (Minneapolis: Fortress, 1998), pp. 83-92.

salem to the ground and against rapacious neighbors? How long must good people endure such affront? These shortest of all questions, "Why?" and "How long?" punctuate four of the psalms (74, 79, 80, 82). Similarly, appeals to divine memory echo the sacred traditions about the permanence of a mutual bond between Yahweh and the people of the covenant.

Even the problematic situation of the northern kingdom occupies center stage in one psalm (80, with an opposite view of this people expressed in 78:67). The image of the Lord of Hosts, an epithet employed five times in this brief psalm, as a shepherd adds pathos to the sense of abandonment, all the more perplexing in light of the care with which the precious vine was transplanted from Egyptian soil and allowed to grow freely. Now that the wall protecting the garden has fallen into disrepair, the wild animals trample it, a powerful image for an afflicted Ephraimite kingdom (cf. Isa 5:5). Instead of grapes and wine, these descendants of Joseph eat and drink tears. Alone among the psalms of Asaph, this one uses a refrain three times: "Lord God of Hosts, restore us; let your face shine on us and rescue us" (80:4, 8, 20, with variable divine epithets).

Different responses to the vexing question of divine justice surface in these psalms: (1) suffering is a test of loyalty (73); (2) adversity was brought on by waywardness (78:10, 37); (3) God controls the clock, choosing precisely the right moment to make a move (75:3); (4) the Lord remains true to the divine nature as revealed to Moses, specifically compassion (78:39); and (5) divine presence compensates for perceived wrongs (73). Only one of these responses exonerates the deity by placing blame on human shoulders; the other four offer hope by appealing to the character of Yahweh. Where humans are culpable, the possibility of an about-face by sinners is held out: "If my people would listen . . . I would feed them with the finest wheat and satisfy them with honey from the rock" (81:14, 17).

The brutal attack on Yahweh's sanctuary, conveyed in a picture of woodsmen hacking down a forest (74:5), left a haunting memory, one intensified by mystification over how Yahweh could allow the divine residence to go up in flames. This humiliation at the hands of foes stands in sharp contrast with ancestral belief that God had conquered the mythic beasts who spawned chaos, subsequently establishing an ordered universe (74:12-17). The taunts by victorious soldiers are understood as directed at Yahweh, who is called upon to defend the deity's reputation, rather than adopt a Napoleonic pose with concealed hand (74:11).

A ruined temple also put an end to the sacrificial cult. What effective means of atoning for transgression remained, now that the daily offerings had ceased? Providing a rationale for the new situation fell to the author of Psalm 50. Here God adopts the position of judge, warning those who harness their tongues to deceit that mere profession of loyalty to the covenant will not drown out the loud voice convicting them of adultery and slander. Faithful adherents to the covenant are assured that God has no need for sacrifices, inasmuch as the cattle on a thousand hills belong to the deity. Therefore God hungers for obedience to the covenant, not for morsels of meat and sips of drink offerings. Praise here replaces the sacrificial offerings and motivates the deity to avenge all wrongs. Here lie the probable beginnings of the synagogue and its substitution of prayer for the sacrificial cult.

Divine constancy has begun to lose its persuasive power (77), causing internal angst for those whose memory is active. The question of longevity surfaces now: Will divine forgetfulness last forever? Or is the present lack of compassion a momentary lapse? Does Elyon (Most High) now resort to a weakened left hand? Recollection of a majestic theophany featuring the God of the storm gives context to the psalmist's consternation over the deity's inactive right hand.

The gem in this collection (73) tests the credibility of a creedal affirmation: "Truly El is good to the upright, Elohim to the pure in heart" (v. 1). On the surface, it seems that the statement contradicts daily experience, where the wicked appear to thrive. The psalmist confesses that this seeming disparity between creed and reality almost led to disloyal thoughts and conduct. A careful assessment of the mind (Hebrew "heart," a thematic word in this psalm) while in the holy place (v. 17) banished bestial thoughts and provided assurance that divine justice would prevail in the end. Thus comforted, the psalmist meditates on the way the divine hand guides into a realm that can only be described with stammering tongue. By this inarticulate language, does the psalmist allude to a blissful state beyond the grave? That question cannot be answered with certainty, although three things seem to indicate an affirmative answer: the strange use of "Afterwards (God) will receive me into glory" (v. 24), with its obvious allusion to Enoch and Elijah; the metaphor of God as rock, indicating permanence; and the reference to a perpetual inheritance. The sublimity of this recognition that only God matters in heaven and on earth seems matched by a sense that even death will not put an end to this close relationship.

Similarities between the rebellious refugees fleeing Egyptian bondage and the victims of Babylonian savagery lead to an exercise in productive memory as a psalmist narrates events of old (78). The crucial issue comes to expression in interrogative form: "Can El set a table in the wilderness?" (78:19). This long exercise in transmitting sacred tradition across generations, which begins with a fine example of withholding the subject until the end (vv. 3-4), acknowledges human frailty as a worthy reason for divine compassion (78:39). The choice of Judah, Zion, and David is characterized in this way: the deity awakens from sleep, like a warrior overcome by wine, and then acts decisively. This narrative of the past functions as an affirmation that God can effect justice, even though momentarily postponing action. The ark and its sacred site Shiloh may have fallen, but David was chosen to set that right. Analogously, Zion lies in ruins, but that is by no means the last word.

The descriptive titles for deity in these psalms range from the generic El and Elohim to the personal Yahweh, with metaphors like rock, judge, savior, and shepherd in between. Elyon occurs in six psalms, with Holy One of Israel attested only once (God of Jacob occurs twice). The Tetragrammaton is absent from only one (82). A decisive progression from the first person plural suffix with Elohim ("our God," 50:3) to the first person singular "my God" (83:14) contrasts with stasis where Yahweh is concerned (50:1 and 83:19), unless the final parallelism of Yahweh and Elyon points to a subtle contrast: Yahweh is God of gods in the heavenly realm (50:1), and Yahweh is Elyon over the whole earth (83:19).

The intimate piety signified by these personal pronouns achieves remarkable warmth despite a perceived absence of mediation through prophecy (74:9). Divine speech is imagined, nonetheless (50:7-15, 16b-21; 75:3-4, 11; 82:6-7), once introduced by the strange expression "a tongue I do not know I hear" (81:6c [5c]).

Psalms of the Korahites

The twelve psalms attributed to descendants of Korah (42-49, 84-85, 87-88) begin with faint hope arising from profound devotion to God (*'elōhîm*) and end with a sense of complete abandonment by the deity, who is named "Yahweh the God of my salvation."[5] The first two psalms in the collection actually comprise a single psalm, as the refrain in Ps 42:6, 12 and 43:5 indicates: "My soul, why are you downcast, why do you groan within me? Wait for God, whom I shall praise once more, my deliverer and my God." On this basis, one ought really to speak of eleven psalms associated with Korah, whose descendants were, according to 2 Chron 20:19, singers in the temple at Jerusalem.

These psalms differ greatly among themselves. They consist of laments (42–44, 85, 88), an epithalamium, or wedding song (45), an enthronement psalm (47), a so-called wisdom psalm (49), and songs of Zion (46, 48, 84, 87). The several inscriptions acknowledge this variety (e.g., *maskîl* in 42, 44, and 88; but also in 45 with the additional "a love song"; *šîr* in 46; *mizmôr* in 49 and 84; both *šîr* and *mizmôr* in 48, 87–88). The composers of these psalms seem preoccupied with sacred space and time, but they also recognize ways in which ordinary times of grief impinge on one's interaction with the holy.

Unique in the Psalter is the wedding song for an unknown royal figure (45). It opens with a striking comparison of an articulate poet's tongue to an efficient scribe's pen, each in its own manner engraving ideas on an impressionable object, and closes with a promise of an enduring dynasty (vv. 1-2, 17-18). The poem consists of two parts, praise of the groom (vv. 3-10) and praise of the bride (vv. 11-16). If the hyperbolic language does not lose touch with reality, the wedding involves a ruler from Israel and a bride from Tyre. Biblical annals record a union of the northern king Ahab to Jezebel, the daughter of a Phoenician king. That marriage lends plausibility to the sentiment expressed here. Distinctive features of this psalm, the absence of the name Yahweh and the unique use of courtly language identifying the king as god (v. 7) add force to the lavish royal ideology typical of ancient Near Eastern cultures. One notes especially the ruler's obligation to promote truth and justice (v. 5), together with the allusion to the king as lord of his bride (v. 12), an idea that is democratized and mocked in the book of Esther (Esther 1:10-22). The mention of ivory palaces echoes Amos's scathing criticism of prosperous citizens in the northern kingdom (Amos 3:15)

---

5. Michael D. Goulder, *The Psalms of the Sons of Korah*, JSOTSS 20 (Sheffield: University of Sheffield, 1982).

and gains credibility from modern discoveries of ivory inlay at the capital Samaria.

The laments in this collection have two extraordinary features: a claim of innocence (44) and a complete expression of divine abandonment (88). The usual acknowledgment of guilt and expression of confidence in divine rescue are missing from these two psalms, although Psalms 42-43 manage a glimmer of hope and Psalm 85 basks in the light of prospects of personified virtues. The latter psalms call for minimal comment, other than to emphasize their tendency toward abstraction, whether the divine epithet rock or the vision of love, justice, and truth locked in intimate embrace. Significantly, truth rises from below and justice descends from above, that is to say, humans embody fidelity and God exacts justice (85). The composer of Psalms 42-43 urges God to dispatch light and truth to lead the worshipper to the holy mountain. Only then will the mocking question, "Where is your God?" (42:4, 11), lose its sting. Corresponding to the enemies' mockery is the psalmist's own questioning of divine constancy; an earlier period of favor has given way to anger, accompanied by human concern over the duration of divine fury (85:6).

The customary confession of guilt has left no trace in Psalm 44, which likens the people of God to innocent sheep on the way to be slaughtered for the deity's sake. The psalmist cannot suppress the thought that Yahweh has succumbed to sleep, content with hiding the countenance on which the faithful wish to look. This dispassionate stance contrasts starkly with past conduct when God assisted Israel's armies in eradicating the inhabitants of the land and then planted the favored people securely. Now God sells innocent victims for a trifle, as if uninterested in making a profit from the transaction. The eighth-century prophet Amos accused the inhabitants of Bethel of similar criminality, together with complete disregard for the price obtained for Israelite slaves (Amos 2:6-8), and a later prophet Joel noted the cruelty associated with dealing in slave trading, which in his mind will be replicated by Yahweh in an execution of exact retribution for this notorious villainy (Joel 4:6-8 [MT 3:6-8]).[6] The psalmist's bold protestations of innocence are coupled with an affirmation of divine access to the secrets of the human heart. In God's case, ignorance is no excuse, for the people's loyalty to the covenant is an open book.

6. James L. Crenshaw, *Joel* (Garden City, N.Y.: Doubleday, 1995), pp. 181-86.

The Eighty-eighth Psalm addresses Yahweh, using the first person pronoun "my God" in apposition. Such intimacy underlines the pathos evident in the poet's sense of absolute abandonment from above, despite constant pleas for relief. The usual images of submersion in the underground waters gives way to a strikingly frank attempt at bribery. The psalmist argues that veneration does not exist in Sheol; consequently, if Yahweh wishes to hear sounds of praise, quick action to rescue the endangered worshipper is essential. In the end the psalmist recognizes God as the afflicter and names darkness as an old friend. Memory of Yahweh's steadfast love, faithfulness, wondrous deeds, and deliverances only heightens the perception of having been forgotten.

Often called a wisdom psalm because it reflects on the universality of death, Psalm 49 begins with an appeal to those high and low, near and far. The poet makes the obvious point that the wealthy leave their possessions behind at death, although this knowledge brings little comfort in light of the universal decree that everyone must die, both fool and sage. Nevertheless, a basis for hope is found in the midst of this decree. Some interpreters understand verse 15 as just another expression of relief from extreme circumstances, whereas others think the language suggests resurrection from death. The antithesis between the rich who cannot ransom themselves from death's summons and God who ransoms the psalmist from Sheol pales before the clear allusion to God's "taking up" Enoch and Elijah (note v. 16, "For God will take me"). This psalm never broaches the divine name Yahweh, even when soaring to lofty heights. Its use of vocabulary that often forms a cluster in sapiential literature — wisdom (except that the form is plural), understanding, proverb, and riddle (vv. 4-5) — is offset by the two imperatives in verse 1 that echo prophetic teaching and the reference to musical instruments accompanying the instruction, which never occurs in wisdom literature. The metaphor of death as shepherding the dead resounds in irony, one of the few comforts available to the poor who harbor fear in the presence of wealth and power. Hints such as this one point to a chasm between the rich and the poor when this psalm was first composed, a rift far deeper than economical. The refrain in verses 12 and 20 mocks human pomp as ephemeral, given death's universality.

The marked festive mood of Psalm 47 implies cultic use, as do the repeated invitations to join in the shouts of adoration. The reason for this elation is communicated in a vivid image of Yahweh's enthronement as God of gods. The concomitant of Yahweh's sitting on the celestial throne is the authority of Yahweh's chosen ruler over all other earthly kings. For some reason, this psalm evokes the memory of sacred traditions about the patriarchs Abraham and Jacob, to whom the land was promised as an inheritance. A procession involving the ark of the covenant, like that presupposed in Psalm 24, may lie behind this enthronement psalm.

Four psalms in this collection celebrate the incomparable power of the city of Jerusalem to stir the religious imagination (46, 48, 84, and 87). These songs of Zion are more at home in mythic symbolism than in geographic reality. The absence of a river in the actual topography of the city does not prevent the poet of Psalm 46 from describing life-bestowing streams, for such language about a river flowing from beneath the temple southward to the Dead Sea occurs in various descriptions of the eschatological age (Ezek 47:1-12; Joel 4:18; Zech 14:8; Rev 22:1-2).[7] This abandonment of reality in favor of mythic language even makes it possible to refer to the city Zion in the far north, despite its southern location and the use in Ugaritic literature of Zaphon (north) for the sacred mountain of the storm-god Baal (48:3).

In these psalms too are expressed the simple longings of pilgrims to reside permanently in Zion's sacred space like lucky birds roosting near the altars of the temple. Such quality time in Yahweh's courts is a thousandfold better than ordinary time, according to Ps 84:11. Moreover, pilgrims making their way to Zion through difficult terrain enjoy Yahweh's solicitous care, providing water to thirsty throats. Yahweh's power also manifests itself in battle, subduing foes, destroying weapons, and ordering fallen soldiers to be still. Towers, ramparts, and citadels dotting Zion's wall testify to Yahweh's might. Appropriately, epithets such as Yahweh of hosts and the God of Jacob resonate through a refrain in Psalm 46 (vv. 8 and 12, probably also in v. 4).

An exalted sense of pride in citizenship finds expression in Psalm 87, a feeling that being born in Jerusalem gives one superiority over those unable to make this claim. Furthermore, the birth of a person in Zion is recorded by Yahweh in a heavenly scroll, elsewhere mentioned in Exod

---

7. James L. Crenshaw, "Freeing the Imagination: The Conclusion to the Book of Joel," in *Prophecy and Poets*, ed. Y. Gitai, SBLSS 32 (Atlanta: Scholars Press, 1997), pp. 129-47.

32:32-33; Ps 69:28; Isa 4:3; Dan 12:1; and Mal 3:16.[8] This assertion cannot be made of those born outside Zion. The sweeping relegation of natives of Egypt, Babylon, Philistia, Tyre, and Ethiopia to second-class citizenship may indicate an internal struggle to adjudicate claims between natives of Jerusalem and Jews returning from places of exile.

Psalms Attributed to Moses, Solomon, and Ethan

Three more psalms stand out in that each of them has been associated with the name of an individual other than David. The content of Psalm 90, a meditation on the brevity of human existence in contrast with the Creator's eternal being, may have suggested that this psalm be identified with King Solomon, whom weavers of legend regaled as the wisest person in the East. The allusion to Yahweh's being older than the mountains recalls various myths of creation employing the temporal expression "Before" as a refrain emphasizing the radical gulf between time and eternity, created universe and Creator. In Prov 8:25-26 personified wisdom utters similar language to press a claim of exclusivity in the divine presence when the creative drama unfolded. Similarly, the deity's questions addressed to Job from the whirlwind (Job 38–39) use this temporal gap to highlight the vast difference between Creator and creature in regard to power and knowledge. The emphasis on the toilsome aspect of life (v. 10) recalls this theme in Ecclesiastes,[9] and the request for diligence leading to intellectual competence ("a wise heart") accords with wisdom literature generally.[10]

Nevertheless, none of these features actually finds exclusive residence in sapiential literature, for they all belong to common assumptions about mortal existence, whether permeating early stories of creation ("Dust you are, and to dust you must return," Gen 3:19) or prophetic proclamation ("Grass withers, flowers fade; surely people are grass," Isa 40:7). The petition for divine turning in verse 13 ("Turn

8. Shalom M. Paul, "Heavenly Tablets and the Book of Life," *JANESCU* 5 (1973): 345-53.

9. James L. Crenshaw, *Ecclesiastes* (Philadelphia: Westminster, 1987).

10. James L. Crenshaw, *Old Testament Wisdom: An Introduction* (Louisville: Westminster/John Knox, 1998).

about, Yahweh, how long? Have compassion on your servants") characterizes ancient laments, and these complaints occur widely in biblical literature irrespective of genre. The request for future happiness equal to past misery may be grounded in the legal concept of measure for measure *(lex talionis)*, so the connection with wisdom is not very firm. Even the expression "a wise heart" is unusual, and the calculating of a normal life span of seventy years, eighty in rare instances, is unique. Moreover, the idea of Yahweh as teacher, implicit in wisdom literature, becomes entirely explicit in a prophetic text (Isa 30:20).

How did Moses' name commend itself to the individual who chose a superscription for Psalm 90? The well-known story of Moses' intercession with Yahweh to turn from wrath to mercy (Exod 32:12) provides a link between the psalm and him, although the prophet Ezekiel does not include Moses in his list of champions at prayer. Instead, he remembers Noah, Dan'el, and Job as incomparable intercessors (Ezek 14:20). Because psalms such as 1 and 119 extol the numerous positive aspects of torah, one wonders why these are not credited to the lawgiver par excellence.

The association of Solomon with Psalm 72 seems natural, given its concern for royal justice, the reference to emissaries bringing gifts from distant Sheba, and the stress on the vast extent of the king's domain. The pious story about Yahweh's promise to give Solomon the insight he requested for governing the people (1 Kings 3:9) echoes the initial prayer in verse 1, except for the stated reason underlying the petition, prosperity and dominion (v. 4). Solomon was remembered as having asked only for wisdom; the other blessings came as reward for putting the people's well-being above that of the king.

This psalm belongs to the ideology of kingship in that it looks to the ruler for securing the safety and viability of marginalized citizens. It also links the prosperity of society with that of the king and subscribes to the belief that all peoples bring tribute from afar in recognition that they have become recipients of the blessing surrounding the patriarch Abraham. The language of verse 15 evokes that of Gen 12:3. The emphasis in the psalm falls on nature's bounty, especially fruit and grain, as a consequence of gentle rain. The double doxology appended to this psalm, with the unique divine epithet "Yahweh God, God of Israel," is the longest of the four and the only one with an additional comment: "The prayers of David son of Jesse have come to an end."

According to 1 Kings 4:31, Ethan was a famous sage like Solomon. The author of 1 Chron 15:17, 19 remembers Ethan for his musical talents. The latter recollection seems better suited to Psalm 89, which opens with the vow to sing Yahweh's deeds of compassion and faithfulness (v. 2) for all generations but closes with a sense that both have been annulled (v. 50). The first section of this psalm is rooted in the mythic language of the Creator's combat against the monster representing primeval chaos, here called Rahab but also known by its Ugaritic name Leviathan (Lotan) and Tannim(n). This psalm has Yahweh crush the enemy; in another version, preserved in the book of Job, for example, the foe is merely held in check by means of prohibitions. This psalm also celebrates Yahweh's dominance within the council of the gods and subscribes to the theory that kingship is founded on justice. The concept of Yahweh's incomparability, a frequent theme in Deutero-Isaiah, finds expression in verses 7 and 9. The reference to Zaphon probably signifies the geographical scope of rule; in conjunction with Amanus, it points to north and south, rather than the sacred residence of Baal. Tabor and Herman refer to mountains in the north and do not necessarily imply that traditions from Ephraimite tribes are being assimilated to southern tradition.

The mention of an eternal covenant with David in verses 4-5 anticipates a fuller discussion of this theme, but first the psalmist establishes Yahweh's power and special relationship with Israel. The force of the appellative "our king," which modifies "the Holy One of Israel," can hardly be missed. Nevertheless, this king has proved unfaithful to an eternal promise: that a descendant of David would always sit on the throne at Jerusalem. Yahweh and David share a bond that enables the king to address his Lord as "Father" and "Rock" (v. 27). Indeed, David even receives the divine epithet "Most High" (v. 28). Just as Yahweh rules in the council of the gods, David is preeminent among earthly kings. The divine promise to David takes sin into account, but the covenant stands regardless of such disloyalty on the part of David's descendants.

This unlimited grace contrasts with the present situation as perceived by the psalmist. The enemy has prevailed, the throne has fallen, and Yahweh has renounced the covenant. Presumably, the historical events of 586 have pushed the psalmist's faith to the limit. The psalm concludes with a lament, a reminder of life's brevity, and an acknowledgment that the enemies mock Yahweh's anointed. Two questions,

"How long? Will you hide forever?" are balanced by a third, "Where are your ancient promises, Lord?" Together they frame the comment about frail mortals just as the events of birth and death envelop one's brief sojourn on earth.

Hallelujah Psalms

Ten psalms are introduced by the Hebrew word *hallelûjāh*, the imperative of the verb "praise" and its object, a short form of the name Yahweh. Eight of these psalms repeat the superscription at the end (106, 133, 135, 146-150), the exceptions being Psalms 111-112. (Three additional psalms, 115-117, have this expression at the end only, but the textual evidence for these is mixed.) The ten psalms do not form a continuous group, nor do they all belong to a single section within the book of Psalms. One of them concludes the fourth unit (106), and the last five provide an impressive ending to the fifth unit as well as the entire book (146-150). One psalm stands alone toward the middle of its unit (135), and the remaining two occur toward its beginning (111-112). The psalms begin with a long confession of Israel's past history of sin and conclude with the demand that every living thing praise Yahweh.

A sense of national pride rises to the surface in this group, perhaps to offset the heightened awareness of rebellion during the entire sweep of Israel's existence. This apostasy appears all the more odious in light of Yahweh's wondrous deeds beginning at the Sea of Reeds. The psalmist catalogues the numerous offenses, especially forgetfulness that led to tempting God in the wilderness, the opposition to Moses and Aaron, the worship of the golden calf, the limited faith with respect to the promised land, the participation in the idolatrous rites at Baal Peor, the failure to eradicate the peoples of the land, and the resulting idolatry and sexual misconduct (106). This psalm acknowledges the fact of dispersion and insists that God remembered the covenant when the people cried out for help. This conviction empowers the psalmist to pray that those now in exile be returned to their homeland.

The election of Jacob/Israel and choice of priestly ministers Aaron and Levi (135:4, 19-20; cf. 115:9-12) go hand in glove with a recognition that the laws of Yahweh are Israel's special possession. Thus privilege implies responsibility, as the prophet Amos saw with such clarity (Amos 3:2). Even the miserable circumstances of the present do not cancel the hope that Zion's fortunes will be reversed (148:14). The thirteen attributes of Yahweh,[11] particularly the positive ones in Exod 34:6, form the basis for believing that Yahweh will not forget the covenant with Israel. The person who composed Psalm 111 mentions the covenant twice in the span of ten verses (111:5, 9).

The seductive power of idolatry, recounted at length in Psalm 106, comes in for caustic mockery in Psalm 135:15-18 (and 115:4-8). Human artifacts, fashioned from precious ore, remain imitations of reality despite their resemblance to their makers. Eyes, ears, and mouth fail to give sight, sound, or speech (115 adds noses, hands, feet, and throats, all equally functionless). Ironically, those who make such idols and worship them will in the end become lifeless like the works of their own hands. The worship of idols by those who have been fashioned by the deity is doubly ironic. Why should persons created by God bow down to a product of their own making?

This adoration of objects fashioned from gold and silver appears all the more ridiculous in light of Yahweh's creative power and kingship that know no bounds. Supreme among the heavenly beings, Yahweh has demonstrated unlimited majesty in creating the universe and harnessing meteorological phenomena (135:5-7; 146:6; 147:8, 16-18; 149:2). This celebration of Yahweh's care for animals differs from similar poetic exuberance in the divine speeches of Job, where the warrior's horse receives extraordinary praise (Job 39:19-25). The author of Ps 147:10 declares that God takes no delight in the strength of horses; here the viewpoint is entirely anthropocentric, whereas the realm of humankind is almost wholly outside the interest of the poet who composed the speeches from the whirlwind (Job 38:1–40:2; 40:6–41:34). An intermediate position achieves full expression in Psalm 115, which assigns ownership of the heavens to Yahweh and of the earth to Israel (v. 16).

Such high praise of Israel's Lord flies in the face of apparent weakness, an inability to protect the holy residence. Jerusalem has lain in ru-

---

11. James L. Crenshaw, "Who Knows What YHWH Will Do? The Character of God in the Book of Joel," in *Fortunate the Eyes That See: Essays in Honor of David Noel Freedman*, ed. Astrid Beck et al. (Grand Rapids: Eerdmans, 1995), pp. 185-96.

ins, its inhabitants scattered among the nations (147), but Yahweh is at the very moment rebuilding the city, healing the brokenhearted, having strengthened its defenses, and established peace and prosperity. The verb forms, participles and finite verbs, emphasize the interplay of past and present, as if to stress Yahweh's constancy. The psalmist sings about a twofold revelation; Yahweh speaks to the nations through natural phenomena and to Israel in written laws. Yahweh's strength and understanding surpass human ken (v. 5). The imagery is staggering. The same one who nurses the injured to health knows the name of each star and its number in the heavens (147:3-4).

This collection of psalms breathes a simple piety in which deeds of kindness toward the needy receive highest commendation. One psalmist even considers charitable acts and lavish gifts a reliable means of success (112:5, 9), along with lending money graciously. In all acts of this nature, the individual merely imitates Yahweh who exalts the lowly and gives children to barren women (113:9), who establishes justice, feeds the hungry, who frees those in bondage, bestows sight on the blind, and champions the cause of marginalized citizens — the poor, the stranger, widows, and orphans (146:7-9). Who would not bow the knee before this incomparable Lord who looks down from heaven and lifts the poor from the ash heap (113:5, 7)? Small wonder this poet calls on everyone to praise Yahweh (113:3; cf. 150). From east to west, morning to evening, let Yahweh's name be praised. The reference to the sun's rising and setting may indicate geographical and temporal comprehensiveness.

The emotional fervor of this piety carries in its wake a strong desire to exact revenge on those who have inflicted pain on Yahweh's people. Their presence in the shadows can be seen in the nagging question of Ps 115:2, "Where is their God?" The ancient idea of holy war, flourishing once more in the Chronicler's ideology, has seized the psalmist's imagination in Ps 149:6-9. With sword in hand and songs of praise in mouth the pious worshipper marches into the fray seeking to establish justice on earth. This widespread belief in a final act of retribution on earth grew out of the oft-heralded justice of Yahweh. It also reinforced a sense of order in society, without which life was entirely unpredictable and notoriously risky. The conviction that the death of the faithful was too costly in Yahweh's eyes (116:15) reinforced this sense of reckoning.

The decisive reversal of a corrupt societal structure that rewards the strong and ruthless citizens remains in the future, but that dismaying reality does little to dampen the enthusiasm of the poet whose voice we hear in Psalm 150. This rousing crescendo resulting from the union of musical instruments and songs of worshippers brings the collection to a fitting close. Voices raised in praise of Yahweh, musical instruments in the divine service, children of God in sacred space — all these appropriately come to rest in Yahweh and create a resounding echo: hallelujah. In this psalm the word hallelujah occurs ten times (counting the variant *hallelûhû*), reminiscent of the Decalogue. If the verb at the end of verse 6 and the two outside the psalm proper are included, the total thirteen recalls the number of divine attributes according to Exod 34:6-7.

The Composition of the Psalter

How did the book of Psalms originate? How did such a strange mixture of private prayers, royal liturgy, communal songs of thanksgiving and anticipation, and didactic instruction emerge in the worship of the Israelites? Who brought the materials together and for what purpose? What unites the diverse texts other than their distinct character as human words directed toward the deity?

We shall offer two types of answers to these questions pertaining to origin and function. The first solution focuses on the content of various collections, whereas the second proposal concentrates on the use to which the works were put. Claus Westermann begins by noting that the Bible attests to a discrete collection of psalms of a single type, namely, the five laments in the book of Lamentations.[12] He finds further proof of his thesis in the thanksgiving psalms from Qumran, a collection of a single type of psalms in which the poet expresses gratitude to Yahweh for physical and spiritual gifts. Westermann then proposes that the Psalter grew out of several collections of specific types, most of which have remained intact.

The starting point for Westermann is the collection of Ascent psalms in 120-134. Because a unique psalm, 119, precedes this unit, he

12. Claus Westermann, *Praise and Lament in the Psalms* (Atlanta: John Knox, 1981), pp. 250-58.

concludes that the earliest Psalter consisted of Psalms 1-119. In his view, the first and last psalms in this unit gave all one hundred and nineteen a particular emphasis on torah, just as the addendum to the book of Hosea in 14:9 provides an orientation for teaching the prophetic work in the light of wisdom.

Westermann next proceeds to isolate the individual collections in the present Psalter and to offer a hypothesis about their present position in the book. He points to the overwhelming preponderance of individual laments in Psalms 3-41 (the exceptions are 19, 24, and 33) and to the Elohistic collection in Psalms 42-83, with a supplementary unit consisting of Psalms 84-88. In his view both of these collections are enclosed by royal psalms (2 and 89). He thinks the next two small collections, Korah psalms (42-49) and Asaph psalms (73-83), are similarly framed by different types (42-43 and 49 on the one hand, 73 and 83 on the other hand). A Davidic section in which the divine name Elohim occurs (51-72) separates these two collections, and an appendix has been added to them all (84-85, 87-88). Again, a royal psalm concludes the collection of psalms (89).

Westermann thinks the next unit consists of 93, 95-99, and its doxological conclusion, Psalm 100 (the two psalms that precede this unit have no connection with it). Next comes a section of praise (103-107, 111-118, to which should be added 135-136). Within this group, Westermann observes, Psalm 108 is composed from Psalms 57 and 60, Psalm 109 pronounces a curse, Psalm 110 is a royal psalm, and Psalm 117 is the misplaced doxological conclusion to Psalms 111-118. Smaller groups consist of Psalms 140-143, which constitute individual laments, as well as Psalms 138-139 and 145. Westermann believes that Psalms 135-136 belong to the small unit, 111-118, and that Psalms 137 and 144 stand apart as a folk song and a secondary composition, respectively. Finally, in his view, there is a short collection of praise, Psalms 146-150.

Erhard Gerstenberger offers a different explanation for the composition and arrangement of the Psalter.[13] He understands the prayers and sacred songs as a handbook for cultic officials in various synagogal communities. Here he differs from virtually all interpreters, who view

---

13. Erhard Gerstenberger, *Psalms: Part I, with an Introduction to Cultic Poetry*, FOTL 14 (Grand Rapids: Eerdmans, 1988).

the psalms as hymns and prayers for use in the worship associated with the second temple. Gerstenberger rejects the explanation of the Psalter as intended for private study and edification, partly because he thinks most people were illiterate. My own study of ancient literacy supports his claim.[14] Who provided leadership in the local synagogues? Gerstenberger favors the view that lower-rank clergy, the Levites, served in this capacity. They used various psalms to heal dangerous rifts within Israelite society, which became more and more subject to divisions between rich and poor.

The emergence of the Psalter, according to Gerstenberger's scenario, can best be described in temporal stages. During the early preexilic period a few psalms came into being but without recognizable units; in the later preexilic age several collections arose: the psalms attributed to Korah (42-49), the Asaph collection (78-83), psalms about the enthronement of Yahweh (96-99), some hallelujah psalms (111-118), and Songs of Ascent (120-134). The exilic period witnessed the rise of Davidic (3-41, 51-72, 108-110, 138-145) and Elohistic psalms (42-83, 84-89). The fixing of the Psalter into five books, as well as the provision of an overall framework (1-2 and 150), took place during the postexilic period. From 200 BCE to 300 CE the Psalter was read in synagogues as a companion codex of Mosaic law, according to Midrash Ps 1:5 ("Moses gave the five books to Israel, and David gave to Israel the five books of the Psalter").

These two explanations for the composition of the Psalter, its present structure and use, based solely on form critical analysis, illustrate both the strengths and weaknesses of this approach. First, it highlights comparative investigation of kindred texts, making it possible to recognize similarities as well as differences in specific genres. Second, it enables interpreters to probe behind the language of the poetry to the social realities underlying the words. The insights obtained from close attention to modes of discourse and human interaction have opened the book of Psalms to fresh reading and greater appreciation by those who benefit from such study.

Nevertheless, the approach also enables readers to see the dark shadows of uncertainty in scholars' minds and to recognize arbitrary

---

14. James L. Crenshaw, *Education in Ancient Israel: Across the Deadening Silence* (Garden City, N.Y.: Doubleday, 1998).

efforts to give answers when the literature resists any rational explanation for its present shape and content. We can spot trends, tendencies, and orientations, but we cannot always see how they relate to one another in forming a coherent work. That is why all such explanations take the form of working hypotheses, each with a small measure of interpretive value.

FURTHER READING

Goulder, Michael D. *The Psalms of the Return (Book V, Psalms 107–150).* JSOTSS 258. Sheffield: Sheffield Academic Press, 1998.

————. *The Psalms of Asaph and the Pentateuch.* JSOTSS 233. Sheffield: Sheffield Academic Press, 1996.

————. *The Prayers of David (Psalms 51–72).* JSOTSS 102. Sheffield: JSOT, 1990.

————. *The Psalms of the Sons of Korah.* JSOTSS 20. Sheffield: University of Sheffield, 1982.

Grossberg, Daniel. *Centripetal and Centrifugal Structures in Biblical Poetry.* SBLMS 39. Atlanta: Scholars Press, 1989.

Nasuti, Harry P. *Tradition History and the Psalms of Asaph.* SBLDS 88. Atlanta: Scholars Press, 1988.

CHAPTER TWO

Related Psalms

Biblical Psalms outside the Psalter

The presence of the same psalm in 2 Samuel 22 and in Psalm 18 implies that there was nothing to prohibit the use of psalm-like material outside the Psalter. An entire book, Lamentations, resembles the majority of psalms, except that it focuses all its energy on a single calamity, the fall of Jerusalem to Babylonian soldiers in 587 BCE. Here, too, the poetic device of alphabetic arrangement, the acrostic, enhances the range of emotion and assists readers in committing the poems to memory. Within the books of Job and Jeremiah powerful laments demonstrate the extent to which faithful servants of Yahweh felt themselves wronged by their deity (e.g., Job 3; Jer 18:19-23; 20:7-12). They direct their complaints to Yahweh and in so doing manifest extraordinary courage in being so straightforward to one who seems to have turned malevolent.[1]

The mythic imagery and language of Psalm 18 betray considerable Canaanite influence, particularly in the depiction of theophany. Baal's domain has been usurped by Yahweh, who now appears as storm deity and gives victory to the king. The intimacy between poet and deity is

---

1. On the oppressive character of Yahweh, see David Penchansky and Paul L. Redditt, eds., *Shall Not the Judge of All the Earth Do What Is Right? Studies on the Nature of God in Tribute to James L. Crenshaw* (Winona Lake, Ind.: Eisenbrauns, 2000); James L. Crenshaw, *A Whirlpool of Torment: Israelite Traditions of God as an Oppressive Presence* (Philadelphia: Fortress, 1984); and David Penchansky, *What Rough Beast? Images of God in the Hebrew Bible* (Louisville: Westminster John Knox, 1999).

emphasized by the epithets and personal pronoun indicating possession: my rock, my fortress, my deliverer, my refuge, my savior. Distance
and presence coalesce to honor the Creator who descends from the
heavenly temple, shakes earth to its foundations, and rescues the one
who cried for help.

The supplicant was no ordinary person, however, as the psalm makes
abundantly clear. The psalmist claims to be pure, having kept the Lord's
statutes intact. Deliverance therefore is understood as reward for faithfulness, in the same way that defeat has befallen the perverse. Such a bold
assertion, "I am innocent," and affirmation, "The principle of reward and
retribution works," are not typical in the psalms of lament.

Although attributed to David, the psalm has been adapted to later
historical circumstances. It recalls Nathan's promise that Yahweh
would secure the Davidic throne in perpetuity and envisions the subjection of foreigners to Judah. The psalm also engages in religious polemic, asserting Yahweh's uniqueness among the pantheon of gods.
The confession, "He is a shield for all who trust in him" (v. 31), is echoed in the section of Proverbs attributed to Agur (Prov 30:5).

Another psalm, Hab 3:1-19, comes equipped with musical notations
"according to Shigionoth" and "to the leader with stringed instruments."
A theophany gives this psalm its character, together with an unprecedented vow of loyalty in the face of starvation. Unlike Psalm 18 where a
storm approaches from the west, here Yahweh arrives from the southern
region of Teman near Mount Sinai. Moreover, this divine appearance is
not dominated by storm phenomena but by plague and pestilence. The
entire description of sovereignty is bracketed by a poignant reminder of a
divine reputation not borne out in reality and a human promise to remain faithful regardless of external circumstances.

The mythic battle between the Creator and chaos has shaped this
psalm, which mentions Yahweh's trampling the back of Yamm, the
Canaanite personification of evil (along with Mot). Yahweh's appearance evoked widespread adoration — glory filling the heavens, praise
filling the earth. The mountains shook, waters roiled, the deep cried
out, the moon stood still. Riding a victorious chariot, Yahweh wielded
bow and arrows against the wicked dynasty. This vision of divine majesty fuels the poet's hope.

Jonah's prayer embedded in the narrative about a fleeing prophet
(Jon 2:2-9) lacks musical notes but resembles thanksgiving psalms

where a grateful recipient of Yahweh's favor expresses gratitude and praise. The verb for entreaty normally applies where help has not yet arrived, casting suspicion on the originality of this prayer despite its ironical fit. Like so many psalmists, this poet calls out for help when overwhelmed by adversity resembling Sheol's waves. In Jonah's case, the image of tumultuous waters is especially appropriate; however, as the prophet describes his predicament the literal language edges toward symbolic speech.

The longing for another glimpse of the sacred place, together with Jonah's assessment of idolaters, introduces religious polemic where thanksgiving alone seems insufficient. In this instance the holy temple rests on earth and offers a proper setting for the payment of vows. The final declaration that deliverance belongs to Yahweh shimmers with irony when viewed in the context of Jonah's overall conduct and the religious devotion of foreign sailors now directed toward Yahweh.

The thanksgiving song placed in King Hezekiah's mouth (Isa 38:10-20) utilizes a theme found elsewhere in the Psalter, specifically that those persons already residing in Sheol cannot anticipate help from Yahweh, for neither Sheol nor Death can praise the Lord. The imagery for Hezekiah's illness rivals anything in the Psalter describing the human condition. His dwelling has been removed like a shepherd's tent; his life rolled up like a weaver's loom and cut off from its source. These exquisite images exist alongside a more typical expression of death: the savage attack of a lion.

This prayer stresses divine forgiveness with matchless symbolism. Yahweh casts the guilty king's sins behind the deity's back where they become invisible. The gift of life now elicits spontaneous praise: "The living, the living they thank you, as I do today; a father makes your faithfulness known to children" (Isa 38:19). The mention of musical instruments in the next verse belongs to a long tradition of victory songs (cf. Miriam's exuberant praise in Exod 15:21 and Moses' song preceding it in Exod 15:1-18; see also Deborah's song in Judg 5:2-31).

Psalms in the Apocrypha

Another instance of a psalm embedded in devotional legend occurs in the deutero-canonical Tobit. In two instances individuals made miserable by the way their lives have turned out pray for release even if that means death. The aged Tobit, whose acts of kindness in burying the dead have brought nothing but misery, acknowledges the justice of the Lord and begs for mercy rather than punishment for his own sins or for those of his ancestors. In the face of undeserved insults, Tobit willingly embraces death but asks that Yahweh continue to look on him (Tob 3:2-6).

Tobit's niece Sarah utters a similar prayer far away, having been brought to a desperate state by the deaths of seven husbands on their wedding night (Tob 3:11b-15). She, too, cannot bear reproach any longer and pleads with the merciful God to let her die or to grant her a favorable hearing. In Sarah's case guilt plays no role, at least in her own eyes. After the removal of her disgrace, Sarah and her new husband Tobias begin to pray on their wedding night. He blesses God and calls on all creation to do likewise. Recalling the first union of Adam and Eve, Tobias observes that lust is not the basis of his own attraction to Sarah and asks for mercy that will enable the two to grow old together (8:5b-7). Her troubled father Raguel, who had already prepared a grave for Tobias, utters a threefold blessing in which the word bless occurs six times along with three references to mercy and compassion for good measure (3:15b-17).

The safe return of Tobias, with bride in hand, prompts his father Tobit to offer thanksgiving (Tob 13:1-17). In some ways this song resembles the psalms of Zion, although Tobit's hope for a restored Jerusalem exceeds anything there. Like the unknown author of Isa 54:11-14, Tobit thinks of a city made resplendent by an abundance of precious gems, an idea that recurs in Rev 21:9-27. A prophetic element also appears in the appeal to turn back in the hope that Yahweh will have pity on the chosen people scattered in exile (cf. Amos 5:15 and Joel 2:12-14). Although Tobit refers to Yahweh as father, he allows the term king to dominate his thought.

To celebrate her victory over the Assyrian overlord Holofernes, Judith sang enthusiastically while the grateful people accompanied her (Jth 16:1-17). Here the reference to musical instruments and dancing women, as well as a new psalm, introduces the description of Judith's heroics that begins and ends with praise of the Lord. The Assyrians' boasts equaled their muster of troops that overran the terrain, but Yahweh used the seductive charms of a woman to foil them — not young men, nor Titans, nor giants but a woman. The psalm calls on all creatures to serve their Maker, who spoke them into being and enlivened them with the spirit. A veiled attack on the sacrificial cult in favor of fear of Yahweh concludes the song, together with a warning to any future enemy.

Besides being a wise teacher, Ben Sira demonstrates his ability to compose psalms of thanksgiving (Sir 39:16-31; 51:1-11). He encourages the combination of joyful singing and instrumental music, although the subject matter resembles religious polemic. A mathematical mind calculates the logical manner by which aspects of creation work to benefit virtuous people but to afflict the wicked, an idea that is developed further in Wisd of Sol 16:24–19:22. A formula of debate, "No one can say . . ." permits Ben Sira to articulate proscribed thoughts and to register disagreement, and formulaic pieces appear here in expanded form. For instance, the four necessities of life in Sir 29:21 (water, bread, clothing, house) have grown to include fire, iron, salt, milk and honey, and wine and oil, with the curious omission of a dwelling place. Similarly, the familiar dreaded foes — famine, sword, and pestilence — in Jer 14:12 are here accompanied by fire, hail, fangs of wild animals, scorpions, and vipers. The prayer in Sir 51:1-11 is similar to many psalms that register thanksgiving for deliverance from the effect of slander that has pushed the poet to the brink of Sheol. Confronted by lies that have reached the ruler, Ben Sira successfully appeals to Yahweh the merciful father and sings the praises of his deliverer.

In the Greek text of the book of Daniel between 3:23 and 24 a national lament and a hymn of praise have been added. The former, the prayer of Azariah, purports to be spoken from inside the flames of a furnace. It includes a confession of guilt that has brought Yahweh's just punishment on Jerusalem and its citizens now in subjection to enemies (cf. the prayers in Daniel 9, Ezra 9, and Nehemiah 9), but also a plea for merciful acceptance of humble trust in lieu of sacrifice and ordained leadership. The hymn of praise attributed to the three Jews in the furnace recalls Psalm 136 in its use of antiphonal refrains. The call to universal praise resembles Psalm 148 but develops the theme much more fully. In unison with all those summoned to praise Yahweh, the three men give thanks for deliverance from the fire. Praise begins with the heavenly beings and celestial phenomena, moves on to atmospheric features, then to earth and its creatures, ending with the young men.

According to 2 Chron 33:18-19 the notorious King Manasseh eventually repented and prayed for forgiveness. The Greek text supplies an appropriate prayer and by doing so bears testimony to Yahweh's mercy comparable to divine justice. Like most prayers of the period, this one is compiled of biblical quotations that stress Yahweh's complementary attributes of justice and compassion as made known to Moses in Exod 34:6-7. Unlike the three patriarchs Abraham, Isaac, and Jacob who needed no repentance, Manasseh acknowledges his egregious past and begs for forgiveness. Bending the knee of the heart, he relies on Yahweh's forgiveness and promises continual praise. The prayer concludes with a doxology, like the several collections of Psalms.

Psalms 151–155
(Additional Psalms of David)

Five additional psalms credited to David have survived in fragmentary form.[2] The first three were inspired by the narrative in 1 Sam 17:1-58 about the youthful heroics of Jesse's youngest son. Psalm 151 refers to David as smallest among brothers but touts his courage in overcoming lions and bears and in slaying the Philistine champion Goliath. The next psalm views the threat to David as real and includes a fervent prayer for deliverance from beasts. Psalm 153, an expression of thanksgiving, presupposes a positive response to the earlier prayer. In typical fashion, the psalmist uses the image of rescue from Sheol with reference to the beasts. Psalm 154, which asserts that the Most High accepts praise as a substitute for voluntary or mandatory offerings of meal and meat, urges people to associate with good companions and to meditate on the law of the Most High, who redeems the poor ones of Jacob. The final psalm recognizes sin's pervasive sway and asks for instruction in the law. The idea of avoiding something that is too difficult echoes a similar sentiment in Sirach (3:23), as does the prayer for deliverance of the elect ones (Sir 36:1-22).

---

2. James H. Charlesworth and J. A. Sanders, "More Psalms of David," in *The Old Testament Pseudepigrapha,* vol 2, ed. James H. Charlesworth (Garden City, N.Y.: Doubleday, 1985), pp. 609-24.

The Psalms of Solomon

Eighteen psalms associated with the name Solomon have survived in Greek or Syriac, although originally composed in Hebrew.[3] They reflect the crisis within Jerusalem resulting from a shift in power, first initiated by internal conflict and then inaugurated by Roman soldiers under Pompey in 63 BCE. The psalms deal with the problem of divine justice and offer various responses, not all of which are consistent: justice is temporarily delayed, suffering is a test, things will be set right in this life at the eschaton, bodily resurrection will resolve the problem. A moral principle of reward and retribution functions here, but so does messianic hope along with an astonishingly open call for political revolution, in this respect resembling the *War Scroll* from Qumran. Although the covenants with Abraham and Moses are mentioned, the one involving David clearly takes pride of place in the psalmist's mind. The conscious imitation of the Davidic Psalter, including the expression *selāh* for a pause in numbers 17 and 18, does not prevent a mixing of types and weakening of parallelism.

Traditional teachings such as the linking of success with virtue (#1) appear alongside specific reference to the death of the Roman general Pompey in Egypt (#2). The powerful attraction of sex with a beautiful woman prompts the psalmist to pray for strong external discipline that will render her appeal ineffective (#16). A cruel punishment for hypocrisy involving adultery is envisioned — having eyes pecked out by crows (#4). Like many biblical laments, these psalms express anxiety over the malevolent tongue (#12). The recurrence of this theme may reflect the fact that in ancient courts the testimony of accusers weighed heavily against the accused.

Several psalms indicate conscious reliance on sacred texts, either to teach a moral or to ask God to fulfill ancient prophecy in their own day. The prayer in the sayings of Agur[4] preserved in Prov 30:1-14 ("Empty, lying words keep far from me; give me neither poverty nor riches; tear

---

3. R. B. Wright, "Psalms of Solomon," in *The Old Testament Pseudepigrapha*, vol 2, ed. James H. Charlesworth (Garden City, N.Y.: Doubleday, 1985), pp. 639-70.

4. On prayer in wisdom literature, see James L. Crenshaw, *Urgent Advice and Probing Questions: Collected Writings on Old Testament Wisdom* (Macon, Ga.: Mercer University Press, 1995), pp. 206-21, and for prayer in the Old Testament, see Samuel E. Balentine, *Prayer in the Hebrew Bible: The Drama of Divine-Human Dialogue* (Minneapolis: Fortress, 1993).

off for me my allotted bread, lest I be full and lie and say, 'Who is the Lord?' or lest I be destitute and steal, sullying the name of the Lord," vv. 8-9) is echoed in the observation that moderately rich people are happy because they are not forced into sin (#5). The sharp opposition between sinner and righteous with respect to conduct and destiny that characterizes Psalm 1 gives rise to the statement that virtuous people search diligently to expose their own unintentional sins, whereas evil individuals add sin to sin (#3). Deutero-Isaiah's exquisite description of nature's response to returning exiles evokes a call to witness the event and a prayer for the Lord to bring the captives home now (#11). The concept of divine discipline occurs frequently, whether in the form of a sharp blow like goading a horse to go in a particular direction (#16) or a parent's gentle hand wielded in secret to protect a person from humiliation (#13). The psalmist welcomes Yahweh's discipline but wishes to avoid the harsh punishment of Gentiles (#7). Those persons who fall under Yahweh's discipline are thought to be happy, inasmuch as the Lord is both just and holy (#10). The descendants of Jacob can rely on the attentive care of Yahweh, whose eyes and ears are attuned to the beloved son, the Messiah (#18).

The abrogation of the divine promise of uninterrupted rule in Jerusalem by a descendant of David does not precipitate a crisis for the psalmist, who freely places the blame on sinful Israelites (#17). Nevertheless, a prayer for David's return to drive out the Romans does not seem inappropriate to this ancient poet. Surely the Lord who arranged and ordered the countless stars can set things right on earth. Even if evil continues to hold the upper hand, the psalmist promises communal faithfulness (#5). The basis for this profound expression of loyalty under any circumstance is clearly stated: although humans act out of kindness sparingly, Yahweh does so often (#5).

On the one hand, the psalmist claims that nothing harmful can befall good people (#13). On the other hand, foreigners have desecrated the holy place, exiled or murdered Jacob's descendants, and made criminality a way of life (#17). Even though the altar is unclean, devout Israelites can offer Yahweh the fruit of their lips (#15). In contrast to those Israelites in Egypt whose foreheads bore the sign of blood, the people now destined for destruction bear a mark on theirs (#15). The New Testament also refers to an identifying mark of the Antichrist on individuals destined for ruin.

The Thanksgiving Hymns from Qumran

The discovery of a scroll containing about twenty-five hymns of thanksgiving in Cave 1 at Qumran further confirms the remarkable vitality of the tradition of psalm writing in the intertestamental period.[5] Cave 4 yielded seven additional manuscripts of this collection, and numerous small fragments of psalms have survived. The title given to these hymns, *Hôdāyôt,* is a noun form of the verb for giving thanks, which occurs often in the introductory line ("I give thanks to you, O Adonai"; occasionally, the variant "Blessed are you" appears in the opening verse). The scroll extends to eighteen columns, often in poor condition and making interpretation difficult.

The psalms fall into two distinct groups. In one group, the speaker claims to be a recipient of extraordinary insights into heavenly mysteries, complains about ill-treatment at the hands of vicious enemies, and enjoys the esteem of a special band of followers. This exalted ego boasts about being raised to a state of communion with heavenly beings (iii 19-29) and insists that the law is engraved on his heart. He accuses his antagonists of celebrating festivals of folly and mouthing smooth things. In another group of psalms, the ego seems communal and the experiences typical.

The setting for the composition was one of sharp conflict between competing religious parties. The language of one psalm suggests that some people had sold out their convictions for economic gain and political power, at least from the perspective of the writer (xiv 20). The psalmist feels persecuted by many foes but enjoys divine protection from the threat of lions. The story of Daniel's rescue in the lions' den provides the language for deliverance from human attackers.

This practice of borrowing images and language from biblical literature indicates considerable familiarity with sacred tradition. The psalmist describes himself as one possessing an instructed tongue (Isa 50:4), quotes a portion of the ancient creed about Yahweh's attributes (Exod 34:6-7), cites Jeremiah's observation about the divine word being shut up in his bones (Jer 20:9), alludes to the mythic tradition of a flaming sword guarding the garden of Eden (Gen 3:24), reflects on the

5. A. Dupont-Sommer, *The Essene Writings from Qumran* (Cleveland and New York: The World Publishing Company, 1962), pp. 198-254.

human condition as lowly clay (Psalm 8), anticipates the coming ruler in Isaiah 11, divides human beings into good and evil and compares them to trees next to a stream or beyond its reach (Psalm 1), contrasts former things with new events (Deutero-Isaiah), and much more.

A strong sense of predestination runs through the psalms, along with an acknowledgment of human choice. The Creator's providential care from infancy to old age is celebrated in one psalm with a warmth of feeling that rivals anything in the Bible (ix 29-37). Here even divine punishment is understood as paternal discipline, giving evidence of the vast scope of God's mercy. Human sinfulness, seemingly universal, does not place such weak creatures outside the grace of God. As in the Bible, so here too, an emphasis falls on human culpability. No one is righteous before the Most High God, the favorite divine epithet in these psalms.

Striking similes emphasize security in the midst of danger. The psalmist compares his experience to that of a sailor (or a ship) in treacherous waters. Alternatively, he likens himself to a bird driven from its nest and to a frightened person entering a fortified city and hiding alongside a wall. The achievement of safety is compared to an infant's lying near its mother's breast. Metaphors enhance this feeling of well-being. God is called a rock, and devout people are held in a bundle of the living. None compares with this rock, not even the other gods. Besides the Most High God, there is nothing.

The people of the covenant define themselves as poor and needy, orphans who enjoy divine protection. The eye of God watches over their souls, despite prophets of falsehood who seek to lure them astray. Occasionally exhortations function to provide courage and motivation for adhering to the narrow path.

These psalms exhibit no concern to place David in the role of author. They breathe a new spirit, one deeply influenced by Persian Zoroastrianism: the wandering eye of the deity; the strong notion of predestination, together with the spirits of good and evil; and the opposing messianic figures (iii 7-18) that have elicited much speculation among modern interpreters. The psalms also make exclusive claims with respect to esoteric knowledge, divine mysteries now in the possession of the leader of the covenanted community. Resemblances to Hellenistic gnosticism have often been noted.

The combination of heart and head, feeling and intellect, gives these thanksgiving hymns a special quality. The psalmist believes that God has shown favor to him and his disciples, eagerly anticipates the victory of the pious over the wicked, and awaits the everlasting light of dawn without any darkness. The very thought that creatures of clay are destined for such favor constantly evokes an expression of grateful awe.

Hymns in the New Testament

A conservative list of specific verses or connected verses from the book of Psalms that are cited directly in the New Testament has been estimated at sixty-nine.[6] From various references to the singing of psalms by early Christians it is clear that hymnic praise linked the new community of faith to its ancestral tradition. The Magnificat (Luke 1:46b-55), Mary's song in response to the angel's revelation of her unique role in the divine plan, draws inspiration from Hannah's expression of grateful praise. Nothing in Mary's song refers specifically to her pregnancy or to the wondrous child in her womb. Instead, she seems content to allude to Yahweh's favor for a lowly servant and to its consequence. For the rest, she sings a victory song extolling Yahweh's strength that brings reversals in society so that the lowly and hungry experience divine favor. This decisive reversal of fortune is seen as the long-awaited fulfillment of Yahweh's promise to Abraham.

The composers of early Christian hymns about Jesus did not show such reluctance. The hymn in Phil 2:6-11 understands the incarnation as self-emptying, a giving up of status rather than grasping for it. That act of self-abnegation, which led all the way to the cross, resulted in exaltation. God bestowed on Jesus a name unparalleled in the universe, one that renders all others as subjects in need of bending the knee and confessing his lordship. Still, as the author sees it, the Son's exaltation does not come at the Father's expense.

Another early Christian hymn, Col 1:15-20, echoes hymnic praise of wisdom as the firstborn of all creation (Prov 8:22-26; Sir 24:9). The same claim is made of the word in John 1:1-3. The hymn in Colossians stresses God's invisibility and understands the Christ as the agent of

---

6. Robert G. Bratcher, ed., *Old Testament Quotations in the New Testament* (London, New York, and Stuttgart: United Bible Societies, 1987).

creation and its cohesive ingredient. As head of the church and the firstborn of the dead, Jesus has attained preeminence. Moreover, the author insists, God chose to dwell fully in him and by the cross to make peace in the cosmos.

FURTHER READING

Charlesworth, James H., and J. A. Sanders. "More Psalms of David." In *The Old Testament Pseudepigrapha,* vol 2, ed. James H. Charlesworth, pp. 609-24. Garden City, N.Y.: Doubleday, 1985.

Dupont-Sommer, A. *The Essene Writings from Qumran.* Cleveland and New York: The World Publishing Company, 1962. See esp. pp. 198-254.

VanderKam, James C. *The Dead Sea Scrolls Today.* Grand Rapids: Eerdmans, 1994.

Wright, R. B. "Psalms of Solomon." In *The Old Testament Pseudepigrapha,* vol 2, ed. James H. Charlesworth, pp. 639-70. Garden City, N.Y.: Doubleday, 1985.

PART II

APPROACHES TO PSALMS

CHAPTER THREE

The Psalms as Prayers

U ntil the rise of modern historical criticism in the nineteenth century, readers of Psalms were primarily interested in them as re-
sources for the devotional life. Within both Judaism and Christianity
religious leaders viewed the individual psalms as genuine prayer, although some Jewish interpreters resisted the attribution of such religious insight to human beings. For them, the decisive issue reflected
one's understanding of Scripture. Did the Bible's content originate
with God or with mortals?

Jewish Interpretation

For Saadiah Gaon (882-942 CE), the book of Psalms was a second Pentateuch, that is, God's words transmitted by David to the people in the
same way Moses was believed to have passed along divine legislation.[1]
The commandments and admonitions in the Psalter merely assumed
the rhetoric of prayer and petition, in Saadiah's view; hence Psalms was
never intended to serve as the prayer book of Israel. For him, ten historical devices and five basic forms of speech (direct address, interroga-
tion, narrative, commandment and admonition, and prayer and petition) yielded eighteen rhetorical modes. Ignoring these stylistic

1. Uriel Simon, *Four Approaches to the Book of Psalms* (Albany, N.Y.: SUNY, 1991). My
discussion of Jewish interpretation depends on Simon.

features caused interpreters like Moses Ibn Giqatilah (eleventh century
CE) to view Psalms as human petition, according to Saadiah, who opposed such a reading because he wanted to defend the prayers of later
sages as the primary liturgical source for the religious life.

Some Jewish interpreters believed that the psalms were prophetic
prayers and poems. Salmon ben Yeruḥam (tenth century CE) subscribed
to the former view, Moses Ibn Giqatilah to the latter. Yefet ben 'Ali (tenth
century CE) went even further than Salmon, insisting that the psalms
were perfect in form and content. By linking seventeen psalms to the preceding one, Yefet rescued them from anonymity. Against Saadiah's defense of the Eighteen Benedictions, he noted that the Holy Spirit had departed long before their composition. His claim accorded with the view
that the Holy Spirit began to inspire humans in Moses' time and ceased
doing so in Ezra's. In Yefet's view, prophetic vision empowered the author of Psalm 137 to see the later Babylonian mockery of exiled Judeans.

Moses Ibn Giqatilah demurred, viewing many psalms as exilic and
denying that anonymous psalms derived from David. In his view, the
psalms address God and therefore do not belong in the prophetic and
sacred poetry. He distinguished between the Holy Spirit and the prophetic spirit and dated most psalms in the Davidic era. Ibn Ezra discov-
ered no principle of arrangement and considered haphazardness proof
of their authenticity. Editors, he thought, transmitted the psalms just
as they found them. In this respect he differed with Saadiah, who believed the psalms had been arranged on the basis of certain principles:
when they were sung, special times, and levitical families to whom they
were assigned, perhaps topically also.

Christian Penitential Psalms

Christian interpreters emphasized the petitionary component in the
psalms, viewing them as expressions of need in moments of crisis.[2] The
prayers came to be used in daily spiritual exercises, eventually becom-
ing standardized according to calendrical holy times. Readings in

---

2. William L. Holladay, *The Psalms through Three Thousand Years: Prayerbook of a Cloud
of Witnesses* (Minneapolis: Fortress, 1993); and Rowland E. Prothero, *The Psalms in Human
Life* (New York: E. P. Dutton and Company, 1905).

Psalms were scheduled to lead worshippers through the entire book within a prescribed period. Some psalms were chosen for special circumstances; seven penitential psalms were identified by the seventh century CE (6, 32, 38, 51, 102, 130, 143). These psalms led supplicants through confession of sin to forgiveness, and beyond that to renewed praise of God. The nature of the offenses remains obscure, probably to strengthen the psalms' appeal to all who sought pardon.

The mood of these penitential psalms, although somber, reaches moments of surprising exuberance. Indeed, one psalmist declares the forgiven sinner "happy" (32:1-2). The danger posed by unconfessed sins gives impetus to an open acknowledgment of all wrongs, but this admission does not rule out the possibility that punishment exceeds guilt in some instances (38:19-21). For this reason, the present moment becomes the time for pity (102:14) inasmuch as no one can stand before God who takes note of every infraction of rules for behavior (130:3). The frequent request for instruction is interrupted on one occasion by an eager editor who offers advice: "I will instruct you . . . Be not senseless like a horse or mule . . ." (32:8-9).

A Different Pattern of the Religious Life: Torah Psalms

At least two psalms propose an alternative to the customary pattern presupposed in the penitential psalms, specifically sin followed by confession. The first psalm introduces the book and answers the important question: "How can anyone be happy?" The key to happiness consists of both a negative, shunning the wicked, and a positive, meditating on Yahweh's teachings, perhaps by reading them aloud. By avoiding evil persons bent on causing injury and by letting thoughts dwell on the *tôrāh*, one can rely on divine favor. The precise meaning of this Hebrew word can not be determined. It may refer to Yahweh's teaching generally, or it may designate the first five books of the Bible.

The simile for happiness, trees planted alongside abundant waters, echoes a similar teaching in Genesis and in Egyptian wisdom literature. Its power derives from the notion of life as depicted in a tree, an idea carried even further in the concept of family trees. When Job contrasted the potential of a fallen tree for rebirth with the hopelessness of mortals, for whom death is final, he employed this symbolism to communicate the gravity of his own situation.

The image representing the destiny of the wicked emphasizes rootlessness, the inability to resist the pull in every direction. Driven hither and yon like chaff before the wind, sinners vanish into thin air, but those whom they mocked dwell securely, for Yahweh loves them. The Hebrew participle *yôdēaʿ* extends beyond a cognitive sense to one of intimate favor. In this psalmist's worldview no gray areas exist; people belong to one category or the other: good or evil. Those in the former group bear fruit; those in the latter group come to ruin. Given the preponderance of laments in the psalms that follow, such an introduction seems remarkably simplistic, almost Pollyannish.

The three verbs in verse 1 (walk, stand, sit) strive for completion, as do the temporal expressions in verse 2 (day and night). Similarly, the three terms for sinners function as an exclusive classification. Opening with joyous promise, the psalm closes with a threat. As in Deuteronomy, life and death lie in the balances, and all individuals choose one or the other (cf. Amos 5:14). The emphasis of the final verse falls on conduct *(derek)* rather than persons; here behavior determines destiny. The initial verse, however, does not interpose an expression denoting conduct between blessing and the individual, even if it proceeds to make action the decisive factor in the divine-human relationship.

Another psalm that attenuates the extreme concentration on sin and its consequences juxtaposes two scenes almost as different as Psalm 1. The Nineteenth Psalm probably combines a traditional hymn to the sun god (19:1-7) and a Yahwistic poem about the joys of torah (19:8-11), to which a personal response has been added (19:12-15).[3] The opening enigma, silent praise of El's splendor by the universe itself, seems to indicate nonverbal communication, unless it suggests that no speech goes unheard. The staple of solar worship, the description of the daily journey of the heavenly disc, evokes thought of energy like that of a bridegroom or a competitive athlete entering a race. Like the sun's heat, El's glory touches everything.

Precisely what work of El's hands deserves such boundless praise? Nature's splendor, which never ceases to amaze the onlooker? Or does

---

3. For a recent analysis of this psalm, see J. Ross Wagner, "From the Heavens to the Heart: The Dynamics of Psalm 19 as Prayer," *CBQ* 61 (1999): 245-61.

something else shine with extraordinary brilliance that surpasses even the sun's dazzling light? The poem about Yahweh's torah identifies the proper subject of spontaneous speech throughout the universe. Using six expressions for divine teachings — torah, testimonies, statutes, commandments, fear of Yahweh, and judgments — and comparing them favorably to the sweetest taste known to anyone and the most precious ore, the poem describes the law's capacity to revive, inform, rejoice, and enlighten. Moreover, the poet asserts, it endures and is altogether just. As in the third guard's speech about women and truth preserved in 1 Esd 4:13-40, which concludes by insisting that truth and its author, God, outlast the sun (vv. 34-40), the psalmist thinks of Yahweh's torah as infinitely greater than the sun.

Sensual language reinforces the intimacy enjoyed between the psalmist and Yahweh. The Hebrew words for the soul (or more correctly, the self), heart, and eyes suggest that the torah renews one's inmost being, bringing joy to the emotional center and health to the eye. The predicate adjectives describing the torah include completeness, reliability, fairness, purity, cleanness, and integrity. These terms combine moral and ritual concepts. Not satisfied with a mere categorizing of the teachings, the psalmist personalizes the observations: "Moreover, your servant is instructed by them" (19:12a). Here, as in Psalm 1, the benefits of adhering to a specific way of life are taken for granted, or, as the psalmist expresses it, "in keeping them (Yahweh's teachings) is great reward" (19:12b). Those individuals who composed the laments may have found such optimism devoid of logical foundation.

Even the author of Psalm 19 qualifies the blanket statement in verse 12b; noting the difficulty of avoiding sin, the psalmist prays for deliverance from unintentional faults. The final plea extends beyond words to thoughts; the former ("my words") provides a link with the hymn about the sun in verses 1-7, and the latter (meditations of my mind) echoes the language of Psalm 1. The divine epithets that conclude Psalm 19, "my rock and my redeemer," connote strength and relationship. A poem that begins in the heavens comes to rest in personal pronouns that relate the celestial and terrestrial.

The use of several expressions for Yahweh's instructions also occurs in Psalm 119, the longest in the Bible with 176 verses.[4] It resembles

4. Jon D. Levenson, "The Sources of the Torah: Psalm 119 and the Modes of Revela-

the two just discussed in that its theme involves the torah, but its general tone recalls those psalms where confession comes on the heels of sin. At two points the psalmist complains of a failure of sight due to watching unsuccessfully for Yahweh to fulfill the ancient promises (vv. 82, 123). The poet boldly points out that the time for divine action is at hand, because Yahweh's law has been broken (v. 126). The entire psalm mixes enthusiasm for the law with prayer for help in the face of temptation and mistreatment from contemporaries. The psalm comes closer to lament than to any other category.

Psalm 119 takes the form of an alphabetic poem (an acrostic) with eight verses devoted to each of the twenty-two letters of the Hebrew alphabet. Each of these verses begins with the particular letter being highlighted, and all are treated in proper sequence. Furthermore, each verse (with the exception of 122) has an expression for Yahweh's teaching. In four of these, all eight words occur (words, precepts, commandments, statutes, ordinances, decrees, law, and promise). The resulting artificiality detracts from occasional sparks of poetic beauty: "Open my eyes that I may see wonders in your law" (v. 18); "For I resemble a wineskin in smoke" (v. 83a); "Your word is a lamp to my feet and a light to my path" (v. 105); "Opening your words enlightens" (v. 130a). The overall impression of the psalm, that it wastes a lot of time uttering tautologies, results from the restrictive requirement of positing eight things about torah again and again, from A to Z. The poet definitely does not practice modesty, despite occasional admission of weakness: "I possess more knowledge than all my teachers" (v. 99); "I understand more than the aged" (v. 100). Threats from detractors have become real, provoking the perennial question: "How long must your servant wait; when will you enact justice against those pursuing me?" (v. 84). Grievously smitten, the poet begs Yahweh for life (v. 107).

The psalmist's whole life is consumed by praise for the torah: "At each watch of the night, or awakening at midnight, and extolling Yahweh seven times a day" (v. 164). The happiness of this worshipper unfolds in the presence of adversity, and the twofold promise of bliss

---

tion in Second Temple Judaism," in *Ancient Israelite Religion,* ed. Patrick D. Miller, Paul D. Hanson, and S. Dean McBride (Philadelphia: Fortress, 1987), pp. 559-74; and Will Soll, *Psalm 119: Matrix, Form, and Setting,* CBQMS 23 (Washington: Catholic Biblical Association of America, 1991).

that opens the psalm (vv. 1-2) has far more realism than the solitary promise in Psalm 1. Those who love Yahweh's law have great peace, for nothing can make them stumble (v. 165); although they may stray like lost sheep and be in need of a shepherd's searching eye, they do not forget the commandments (v. 176). Possessing these statutes, the psalmist claims to have all the counselors needed for successful living (v. 24).

Psalm 23

The allusion to the worshipper as a stray sheep echoes the presupposition of perhaps the most familiar psalm of all. In it the emphasis falls initially on the divine shepherd (23:1-4) but gives way to the image of a host (23:5). The metaphor of shepherd had wide use in the ancient Near East with reference to deities and kings. It could express solace, as in this psalm, but the word could entail sharp criticism for failing to administer justice. The Egyptian *Admonition of Ipuwer* (perhaps seventeenth century BCE) rebukes the divine shepherd for dereliction of duty, and biblical prophets recognized this dark side of human leaders (Zech 11:4-17).

The psalmist feels completely secure in Yahweh's protective care. Neither privation nor external threat poses any danger, for the Divine Shepherd provides food and drink in the same way Yahweh was said to have supplied manna and quail for refugees fleeing Egypt under Moses' leadership. By the absolute use of the verb *ḥāsēr* ("to lack"), which always has an object except in Neh 9:21 with reference to Yahweh's provision for Israel's well-being in the wilderness, the poet recalls this momentous event. With full stomach, sheep lie down in lush greenery. When thirsty, they are led to still waters for a drink that restores vitality. In unfamiliar terrain, they are prevented from wandering beyond safe paths, for the shepherd's reputation is at stake. Even were they to travel in a darkened valley, they would rely on the shepherd's rod for defense against predatory beasts and depend on the staff for gentle leadership.

The other image derives from the inner sanctum, in this instance a tent (or possibly a house) into which a stranger has been invited. The importance of hospitality in the ancient Near East can scarcely be overstated. Breach of an unwritten code of protection under one's tent, and by extension house, gave rise to various stories, particularly the episode involving Lot (Gen 19:1-11) and Benjaminites residing in Gibeah (Judg

19:16-30). An egregious example of betrayal by a host, the murder of
the fleeing Canaanite soldier Sisera by Jael the wife of Heber the Kenite
(Judg 4:17-22, also recounted in a poetic version in Judg 5:24-30), has
not led to condemnation of the one who betrayed her guest. Zeal for
Yahweh's cause in battle as perceived by the author has overridden normal protocol.

The psalmist envisions Yahweh as a host who has invited an endangered foreigner to the inner refuge and has prepared a lavish feast, as
Abraham entertained three strangers in Gen 18:1-8. In addition to the
gift of food, the host brings a generous supply of olive oil for the guest's
head, offering relief from the sun's drying effect on skin. The presence
of enemies does not deter the host from fulfilling the obligatory duties.
Instead of pursuit by enemies, the guest anticipates being followed by
kinder agents, personified goodness and mercy. A single visual image
suffices for this section of the psalm: "my cup overflows" (v. 5). By coming to rest in Yahweh the final verse returns to the tenor of both metaphors, shepherd and host: "And I shall reside in Yahweh's house for
days on end" (23:6b).

Reflection on Human Nature

In some ways the most intriguing psalm of all reflects on the nature of
humankind somewhat after the manner of the priestly account of creation in Gen 1:1–2:4a, especially the observation that man and woman,
who bear the divine image, rule over all other creatures. Psalm 8 manages to hold together an exalted view of Yahweh's majesty and a high
estimate of human beings. Neither detracts from the other, although
the psalmist appears to be surprised that the former, Yahweh's awesome splendor, does not erase interest in earthlings.

As frequently occurs in texts of such magnitude, the precise meaning of the language eludes readers. Do the spontaneous praises of infants establish a bulwark that enemies cannot break through? If so,
who are Yahweh's foes? The enemy and avenger, here personified, seem
to be variants of names for the dragon of chaos, otherwise known by
different names such as Leviathan, Tannin, Rahab, Behemoth, Yamm,
Mot, Marduk, and Apophis. This understanding of the text seems to
connect it with the solar hymn in Ps 19:1-7 and with various myths of

creation that emphasize hymnic response to the act of creation (Job 38:7; Prov 8:31). Irony makes the point effectively; the adoring babble of infants erects a protective barrier securing Yahweh from all threat. Can anyone be more awesome than that? If the adoration of suckling babes renders Yahweh invincible, think what an army of warriors would do? That line of argument lies beneath the poet's understatement.

Lowering the eyes to take in creatures under the heavens, the psalmist makes an astonishing assessment of human beings. They fall just short of God — heavenly beings. The Hebrew word *'elōhîm* can have both meanings; here the audacity of the claim favors the sense God. Compared to moon and stars,[5] women and men lack luster. Yet they become objects of Yahweh's attention, here viewed favorably. Indeed, they wear crowns of glory and honor while ruling over all creatures domestic and wild, including fish and fowl. The reference to everything that traverses the sea extends human control to include imaginary dragons and all other foes in the dreaded waters.

The refrain, "Yahweh our Lord, how majestic is your name in all the earth," introduces the adulation of God and concludes the admiring observation about humans (8:2, 10). An artful verification of language occurs outside parallel half lines: "the works of your fingers" in verse 4 becomes "the work of your hands" in verse 7. That reading contrasts with in-line variety such as *'enôš* and *ben 'ādām* to denote humankind in verse 5. The expression for dominance in 8:7b ("All things you have placed under his feet") derives from military action and recalls the images of a king standing on a fallen foe. The verb for ruling over Yahweh's works in 8:7a, *māšal*, differs from that in Gen. 1:26, where *rādâ* seems more forceful. Furthermore, the priestly author's addition to the expected beasts, birds, and fish says nothing about creatures of the sea and restricts itself to creeping crawlers on land.

Not everyone shared the esteem in which human beings were held by this psalmist. The composer of Ps 144:3-4 also asks about human nature but concludes that men and women resemble a breath or moving shadow. The idea that Yahweh pauses to take note of such transience presents an anomaly, and the psalmist refuses to give it a second thought. After all, this low view of humankind was standard fare (cf. Ps 39:6; 102:12; and, with a vengeance, Ecclesiastes).

---

5. Has the Hebrew word for sun (*šemeš*) been corrupted to *šāmēykā*, "your heavens"?

Naturally, the question "What are mortals?" was widespread in ancient Near Eastern literature, but it usually emphasized a relationship of mastery vis-à-vis a subject. A supplicant articulates the question "Who/what am I that . . . ?" and in so doing calls attention to the breach between the two. The poet responsible for Psalm 8 uses the question to reinforce human honor. The unknown author of Job 7:17-21 asks "What are mortals?" but goes on to view God's unwanted attention as menace rather than solace. The linguistic similarities between this text and Ps 8:5 (the question "What are mortals?" and the verb "to visit") may not indicate direct influence one way or the other, and differences stand out (the missing parallel to ʾenôš, the presence of gādal, "to exalt," and the negative sense of divine visitation).

For many readers Psalm 139 goes even further than Psalm 8 in reflecting on the Creator's intimate knowledge of mortals and in its assessment of them. Not only does Yahweh possess sweeping information about the psalmist's conduct and unspoken thoughts, but, for this matter, no haven of retreat from the divine spirit exists, should one even imagine such a thing. The places enunciated here — heaven, Sheol, the farthest sea, and darkness — remind one of the sequel to the fifth vision in Amos 9:2-4. Here the prophet mentions various hiding places resorted to by hypothetical fleeing individuals hoping to escape Yahweh's wrath. He includes Sheol, heaven, Mt. Carmel, the bottom of the sea, and exile, but in Amos's view such remote places could not conceal anyone from Yahweh's gaze.

The psalmist feels hemmed in by the divine presence but welcomes the attention. The difference between this poet's response of incomprehensible wonder and Job's reaction to being hedged in by the deity could hardly be greater. The psalmist may be unable to fathom the mystery of such intimate knowledge by the Creator but views the Hound of Heaven, to use Francis Thompson's language, as comforting. Yahweh's hand sustains rather than punishes; as in Ps 73:24 divine guidance comes when least expected. The psalmist's brief flirtation with escaping divine surveillance, even if only in the imagination, gives way to realism. Even the cover of darkness cannot prevent Yahweh from seeing him and grasping him by the right hand.

The crude depiction of conception in verses 13-16 contains ancient speculation about the deity's role in that process. This kind of thinking occurs widely, for the peoples of various cultures believed that their gods assisted in pregnancy and birth. The precise nature of that contribution by the deities was not clear, but ignorance did not prevent them from trying to describe their activity. Biblical speculation about the process of gestation occurs here and in wisdom literature, especially in Job 10:8-11, Eccles 11:1, and Wisd 7:1-6.

Two things stand out in the psalmist's account: the emphasis on a stage in the earth's womb and the concept of a predetermined life span. If Job's well-known response to his suffering, "Naked I came from my mother's womb and naked shall I return there . . ." (Job 1:21), does not employ the adverb "there" as a euphemism for Sheol, the text may presuppose the notion of mother earth as source and eventual goal. Moses used the idea of a divine scroll on which are inscribed the names of the elect with enormous impact in convincing an angry Yahweh to spare the guilty worshippers of a golden calf. The element of awe surrounds the entire description of the psalmist's origins; verse 14, like verse 6, permits this sense of wonder to find expression and in so doing links the two sections together, the individual's enclosure (139:1-12) and formation (139:13-18) by the deity.

The Cursing of Enemies

The third unit of the psalm (139:19-24) introduces a jarring note for which readers are wholly unprepared, unless the hemming in has actually produced negative feelings like those entertained by Job's Adversary. This remarkable move from ardent intimacy with God to such ferocity results from the psalmist's identification of personal enemies with those of Yahweh. The prayer for Yahweh to kill the wicked grows out of what the psalmist considers perfect hatred, although the final request for Yahweh to determine whether or not wickedness has crept into such thoughts may indicate discomfort over giving free rein to hatred. That seems unlikely, for psalms of this nature occur frequently in the Bible.

According to Norbert Lohfink, "The one praying and his or her enemies — that, in short, is the dominant theme of the Psalter."[6] In it

6. Norbert Lohfink, "Was wird anders bei kanonischer Schriftauslegung? Beobachtungen am Beispiel von Ps. 6," *Jahrbuch für biblische Theologie* 3 (1988): 36.

Othmar Keel counts ninety-four words describing enemies.[7] This extraordinary concentration on enemies led Erich Zenger to observe that "in fact, hatred, enmity, violence, retaliation, and even revenge are not sub-motifs in the Psalter: they are substantive parts of it."[8] What can one say about this obsession with enemies and their destruction? Do such thoughts belong in prayer?

We can quickly dismiss one attempt to deal with the desire for revenge on enemies: the argument that it reveals human nature without Christ. Such a simplistic answer errs in two ways: first, by unnecessarily driving a wedge between Judaism and Christianity, and second, by failing to see the universality of the attitude, including its prevalence in Christendom despite clear teachings to the contrary by its founder. Does the dominical injunction to love one's enemies and return good for harm ignore the larger issue of divine justice by contributing, even if inadvertently, to an unjust law?

Zenger takes this approach to the problem of prayers for revenge on enemies. He thinks that a society devoid of justice indicates a *deus otiosus*, a nonfunctioning deity. It follows, in his view, that religious people have an obligation to take Yahweh's justice seriously and to insist on its implementation at the expense of the wicked. Anything less than this commitment to the dawning of justice on earth Zenger considers a form of cynicism. He writes: "Ultimately, this is the question of theodicy; where the righteous find no justice, God has forfeited existence."[9] Again, "The passion of these psalms arises from the fundamental conviction that justice must be done. . . ."[10] They are, in a word, realized theodicy. By praying that God eradicate the wicked, the psalmists place everything in Yahweh's hands while at the same time voicing a longing for God to speak the last word. Zenger thus understands these prayers for vengeance as affirmation of divine integrity in the face of strong evidence to the contrary.

C. S. Lewis makes a similar point, showing that inability to speak against evil or even to recognize sin may be worse than cursing ene-

---

7. Othmar Keel, *Feinde und Gottesleugner: Studien zum Image der Widersacher in den Individualpsalmen*, SBM 7 (Stuttgart: Verlag Katholisches Bibelwerk, 1969), pp. 93-131.

8. Erich Zenger, *A God of Vengeance? Understanding the Psalms of Divine Wrath* (Louisville: Westminster/John Knox, 1996), p. 13.

9. Zenger, *A God of Vengeance?* p. 37.

10. Zenger, *A God of Vengeance?* p. 67.

mies.[11] At least opposing meanness indicates a conscience. Furthermore, Lewis argues, the act of cursing wicked people forces the speaker to come to terms with hatred, now vocalized. Lewis turns things around to focus on the dreadful wrong committed by sinners who generate hatred in otherwise good people. This kind of reasoning does not lead him to condone the imprecations, for he thinks they come like blasts from the mouth of a furnace. Moral indignation, however, he views as proof that the religious person takes sin seriously as an affront against the Lord and human companions.

Unlike Lewis, Zenger purges the prayers of their irrefutable essence when claiming that the judgment envisioned has repentance as its purpose. His argument that the wicked should be confronted in such a way that they honor justice through repentance has little if anything to do with the request that Yahweh kill the wicked in Ps 139:19 or with the comment in Ps 58:11-12 that the righteous rejoice while bathing their feet in the blood of evildoers because they recognize an act of justice. Apparently aware of this weakness in his reasoning, Zenger remarks that judgment is for the sake of justice, especially for the victims. He quotes Gottfried Bachl that "judgment is the way God helps human beings to self-discovery; it is liberation from the delusion of innocence, awakening from the day of conscience, release from life's lie."[12] When judgment brings about the death of the wicked, how do they find an occasion to repent of such delusion and to know the truth?

Herein lies the complexity of the problem. The effort to circumvent the issue by insisting that wrath does not belong to God's essence but to a role demanded by the divine imperium does not really address the matter. By insisting that Yahweh did not desire anyone's death, the prophet Ezekiel used a form of the argument long before Lactantius. Why should a benevolent deity feel constrained to destroy mortals even for the purpose of restoring order? Proving that God actually functions in the world may not be nearly as significant as demonstrating an infinite capacity for mercy. Must human beings suffer loss of life simply to preserve the divine reputation? Does that name matter if purchased by the blood of mortals? These questions suggest that the prayers for ven-

---

11. C. S. Lewis, *Reflections on the Psalms* (New York: Harcourt, Brace and Company, 1958), pp. 20-33.

12. Zenger, *A God of Vengeance?* p. 68.

geance, although understandable, cannot be justified theologically whether in terms of an altruistic concern for victims of injustice, or defense of divine honor.

Perhaps the strongest objection to such efforts to justify these prayers is the failure to recognize the extent to which religious people tend to identify their own enemies with God's adversaries. The arrogance of such thinking is conceived in pride, possibly a more grievous sin than those offenses that have earned "evildoers" a sentence of death in the prayers of the proud. This self-identification with God's purpose as understood by the pious worshipper shields that person from identifying the signs of spiritual decline. The use of Psalm 109 by Martin Luther and John Calvin to justify pogroms against Jews and others reveals the extent to which this deadly disease can strike religious leaders with its poison. C. S. Lewis has remarked that individuals with enormous potential for good are precisely the most dangerous because they believe so passionately in the justice of their cause. Consequently, they identify their own views with God's intention; in this way, extremism in God's name enjoys the highest sanction of all.

The use of Psalms for daily devotion and as a model of prayer therefore runs the risk of infecting religious people with harmful attitudes. Do the prayers for vengeance against personal enemies sacralize violence? René Girard and his students have explored this phenomenon in a wider setting under the language of scapegoating.[13] The widespread practice of killing an innocent scapegoat for the purpose of restoring order in society undergirds their writings. The innocence of the victim, however, separates their work from the problem under discussion here, for the psalmist implies that the enemies deserve divine punishment.

Metaphors for Yahweh

Do the metaphors for Yahweh throughout Psalms compensate for the problem of these vengeful prayers? According to Thorkild Jacobson, the metaphors for the gods of ancient Mesopotamia evolved over three

---

13. On Girard's views see James G. Williams, *The Bible, Violence and the Sacred: Liberation from the Myth of Sanctioned Violence* (San Francisco: Harper San Francisco, 1991).

millennia from natural images through royal to familial.[14] These three emphases corresponded, in his view, to the eras when society was rural, later replaced by city states, and finally by strong families. Their gods were viewed in terms of society: initially as aspects of nature and hence unpredictable, then as kings with power over life and limb, and eventually as parents.

Royal metaphors occur often in Psalms despite the collapse of the monarchy in Israel and Judah. The temporary demise of the Davidic kingdom did not prevent psalmists from envisioning its return or from recognizing Yahweh as supreme ruler in the same way Isaiah believed that the death of Uzziah did not affect true kingship (Isa 6:1). Similarly, the psalmists described Yahweh as warrior, judge, and deliverer. These metaphors signify royal attributes associated with protecting citizens from external threat and implementing justice in society. In Psalms, however, Yahweh's kingship reached beyond earth to cover heaven as well. Accordingly, the gods were subservient to Yahweh.

Some metaphors emphasized the sense of security enjoyed by worshippers of Yahweh or their hope for protection under the divine wing. The language of refuge and fortress dominates this semantic field, along with the metaphor of rock in the double sense of durability and strength. Other metaphors, deriving from rural existence, depict Yahweh as shepherd and gardener. Still others, such as father and portion, come from the intimacy of the home. Surprisingly, psalmists rarely allude to love for and by God. Only Ps 18:1, the larger context of which bristles with eight metaphors of protection, mentions love for Yahweh, unless Ps 97:10 also refers to human love. The Hebrew seems to suggest Yahweh as the object rather than subject. Otherwise, this text alone mentions Yahweh's love for mortals, here identified specifically as persons who hate evil.

Other emotive terms fill this void, particularly *ḥesed* in the sense of enduring love. Thus, for example, the psalmist in 26:3 remarks: "For your enduring love is before my eyes, and I have walked by your integrity." The idea of mapping one's daily journey by means of Yahweh's truth and of constant vigilance directed at the Lord's steadfast love conveys the extraordinary closeness of the psalmist and Yahweh. The language of majesty has left room for expressions of intimacy.

14. Thorkild Jacobson, *Treasures of Darkness: A History of Mesopotamian Religion* (New Haven and London: Yale University Press, 1976).

A Handbook for Religious Life

Not every psalm belongs to the category of lament, a pouring out of one's need in prayer. Some psalms involve royal liturgy, and at least one is associated with the wedding of a king (45). Others seem to have been composed for and by pilgrims on their way to Jerusalem, and still others for processions during local festivals involving the ark and determining visitors' worthiness to enter a holy place. A few psalms appear to have a learned audience and to function as educational tools. Because of this variety in both form and content, some interpreters characterize the book of Psalms as a handbook or manual of spiritual life.

What were the occasions for this prayer, praise, and instruction? The circumstances underlying the laments were many, including, among others, physical illness; psychological stress resulting from slander; threat from enemies; danger from wild animals; exposure to famine, pestilence, and plague; fear of magical practices such as witchcraft; guilt over sin and the perceived absence of Yahweh; desire for pregnancy and bountiful harvests; and concern for the well-being of rulers and religious leaders. The hymns of praise centered on religious festivals, holy places, and sacred times. The locus of the instruction in the psalms is unclear. Some interpreters argue for the presence of schools within the precincts of the temple, and others insist that teaching was merely one aspect of the training of lay leaders. With these observations, we have moved to a second approach to the book of Psalms, namely, as a resource of historical information about ancient Israelites.

FURTHER READING

Daglish, E. R. *Psalm Fifty-One in the Light of Ancient Near Eastern Patternism.* Leiden: Brill, 1962.

Holladay, William L. *The Psalms through Three Thousand Years: Prayerbook of a Cloud of Witnesses.* Minneapolis: Fortress, 1993.

Kugel, James L. *The Great Poems of the Bible.* New York: Free Press, 1999 (Psalms 23, 29, 42, 51, 104, 119, 137).

Levenson, Jon D. "The Sources of the Torah: Psalm 119 and the Modes of Revelation in Second Temple Judaism," in *Ancient Israelite Religion,* ed. Patrick D. Miller, Paul D. Hanson, and S. Dean McBride, pp. 559-74. Philadelphia: Fortress, 1987.

Lewis, C. S. *Reflections on the Psalms.* New York: Harcourt, Brace and Company, 1958.

Miller, Patrick D. "The Hermeneutics of Imprecation," in *Theology in the Service of the Church: Essays in Honor of Thomas W. Gillespie,* ed. Wallace M. Alston, Jr., pp. 153-63. Grand Rapids: Eerdmans, 1999.

———. "Deuteronomy and Psalms: Evoking a Biblical Conversation," *JBL* 118 (1999): 3-18.

Prothero, Rowland E. *The Psalms in Human Life.* New York: E. P. Dutton and Company, 1905.

Simon, Uriel. *Four Approaches to the Book of Psalms: From Saadiah Gaon to Abraham Ibn Ezra.* Albany, N.Y.: SUNY, 1991.

Soll, Will. *Psalm 119: Matrix, Form, and Setting.* CBQMS 23. Washington: Catholic Biblical Association of America, 1991.

Williams, James G. *The Bible, Violence and the Sacred: Liberation from the Myth of Sanctioned Violence.* San Francisco: Harper San Francisco, 1991.

CHAPTER FOUR ✦

Psalms as a Source of Historical Data

At first glance, the psalms do not look promising as repositories of historical information, for they usually treat typical incidents with general application rather than specific events of limited interest. The exception, the events associated with the departure from Egypt under Moses' leadership, are understood as an exemplary incident to which faithful descendants of these original Israelites look for inspiration and warning. The psalms that recall these historical moments keep alive the memory of foundational events in Israelite origins. The allusive character of the narrative implies an informed audience, for either memory or imagination must supply the details of various incidents. A few references to later historical events occur here and there. For example, Psalm 137 presupposes an exiled Jewish community in Babylonia and depicts the mockery to which it was subjected by the conquering people. Several psalms recall the signal event in the life of Judeans, the capture and destruction of Jerusalem by Babylonian warriors (51, 74, 79, 102) and the devastation of major cities in Judah (69). The plea that Yahweh rebuild the walls of Jerusalem (51:18), sometimes taken as a later gloss, points to the vulnerability of its inhabitants in an exposed environment. Psalm 74 goes into considerable detail about the manner in which the city fell, focusing mostly on the temple and its precincts. With axes, hatchets, and hammers the soldiers destroyed the sanctuary and its carvings, subsequently burning the holy place in Jerusalem and all other sacred sites in the land, a curious statement in light of the Deuteronomistic historian's claim that Josiah demolished those altars decades earlier. The mention of perpetual ruins with reference to Zion emphasizes the extreme misery implied, as does the assumption that prophecy has vanished, leaving the people clueless. The scope of human suffering as a result of Jerusalem's defeat comes to expression in Psalm 79, specifically unburied bodies being devoured by birds and beasts, and blood flowing freely.

The impressive defenses of Jerusalem struck the author of Psalm 48 as worth mentioning, and pride in one's place of birth evokes an incidental comment in Psalm 87 about town records, a rudimentary city registry. Reference to Yahweh registering the people seems to imply human records as the source of the analogy. Scribal activity is surprisingly missing, except in a passing remark about a ready scribe (45:1). Another institution, kingship, receives fuller documentation; it is presupposed in a number of psalms (e.g., 2, 21, 29, 47, 72, 93, 99), along with its symbol, a scepter (89). The activity of judges is mentioned often, although most of the references probably indicate royal protection and deliberation (7).

The historian of warfare finds considerable information in numerous psalms (e.g., 5, 18, 20, 21, 35, 44, 46). These psalms provide data about weapons, in this case bronze swords, spears, javelins, shields, banners, bows and arrows, horses, and chariots. Victorious soldiers took prisoners (68, 102, 107) and demanded tribute from defeated peoples (68, 72). Purchase of enslaved individuals was possible through payment of a ransom (49), a term that assumed a spiritual dimension with reference to divine forgiveness. Slavery occurred as a result of debt as well as warfare (123).

Economists can glean important data from several psalms, particularly indications of prosperity such as ivory palaces (45:8), cash liquidity (15:5), and a mercantile fleet (48:8; 107:23). Rich and poor exist alongside one another, but an easy identification of the rich with evildoers sometimes takes place (52:7; 73:3). Conversely, the poor hope for Yahweh's favor (9:19). The psalmists value precious honey, fine wheat, and the purest gold (19:11; 81:17), and they are familiar with the refining of silver (12:7; 66:10). References to agriculture, mostly viticulture and cultivation of grain (4:8; 65:10; 126:5-6), emphasize Yahweh's role in assuring a bountiful harvest and in bringing joy to replace tears.

Individual psalms provide insight into the development of religion in Israel and Judah, particularly with regard to the cult and its practices. Astonishingly, in light of the frequent references to sacrifices, almost complete silence occurs about priestly officials (110:4, which mentions the enigmatic figure Melchizedek, the subject of later speculation in Hebrews 5-7). Not every reference to the daily offerings recognizes them as valid; they are attacked in Ps 40:7; 50:8-16; and 51:18-19. The importance of vows in daily life can be seen in the many instances in which a worshipper promises to pay vows to the Lord (e.g., 22:26; 50:14; 61:9; 65:2; 66:13; 116:14). The practice of human sacrifice during the wandering in the wilderness and the worship of idols have not been expunged from the record (97:7; 106:37; 115:4-8; 135:15-18), although the idols come in for extensive mockery. The main festivals of the year have to be identified from the contexts, but an irrefutable reference to festivals does occur (42:5). Rites of mourning dictated appropriate clothing, especially sackcloth (30:12; 35:13; 69:12), as well as the systematic preservation of the bones of the deceased in ossuaries (34:21).

Musicologists find a wealth of data, particularly in the superscriptions, which frequently include musical notations about specific tunes, musical score, and the like. Many of these data have yet to be explained, along with certain terms for pauses and so forth. The names of rare musical guilds have survived, as have references to several types of instruments — harps, lyres, cymbals, lutes, trumpets, horns, timbrels (or hand drums), strings, and pipes (33:2; 57:9; 92:4; 98:5-6; 108:3; 149:3; 150:3-5).

The psalms offer considerable evidence to assist zoologists in determining the types of domestic and wild animals throughout the land. We find references to lions and wild oxen, badgers, horses, mules, sheep, and goats. Bears, known from other texts to have been a threat at the time, escape mention. Snakes, adders, and specialists in charming these dangerous creatures do receive notice (58:5-6; 140:4). A few references to the capture of wild animals by means of digging pits over which nets were stretched to ensnare them also occur, but this language refers to catching humans (9:16; 35:7; 57:7).

Occasional allusions to social conventions associated with the land offer useful information. For instance, land could be passed on from generation to generation on the basis of a principle of inheritance (25:13) and in accord with covenantal promises from Yahweh. On two occasions we come upon an allusion to a symbolic gesture of tossing a sandal, which appears to indicate mastery over another person (60:9 and 108:10, here of nations, Moab and Edom). A reference to the custom of anointing the head with oil provides a vivid indication of a psalmist's respect for Aaron (133:2).

The individual psalms also contain vital information about the development of the Hebrew language, its grammar, syntax, and philology. Furthermore, they bear witness to changes in religious thought as seen in mythic characters, especially about the creation of the world through combat with agents who represent chaos, but also about epithets for Yahweh and the struggle to eradicate the worship of idols. In addition, some psalms offer insight into the reuse of liturgical units such as that found in Exod 34:6-7, an enumeration of Yahweh's thirteen attributes (103:8; 145:8). Others provide valuable data on Egyptian influence, whether ideas like righteousness and justice as the foundation of the royal throne or the hymnic tradition (89:15, 19; 104). Priestly control over those persons admitted to places of worship is hinted at in entrance liturgies such as Psalm 15 (cf. also 24:3-4).

This brief discussion of the study of Psalms as historical data could be expanded in several directions, such as the rhetorical and poetic devices in use, the geographical areas and topography of the land, the rivalry among various regions, and the psychological factors at work in the mind of the poets. Even if we examined these matters, the result of the total enterprise would not satisfy many readers. One thinks of a parallel from research into the book of Job. The commentary by Gustav Hölscher, which is restricted to the observable phenomena of religion, covers only 102 pages;[1] a comparison with traditional commentaries reveals the limitation of the historical approach.

Iconography and Psalms

A promising approach to the symbolism in the book of Psalms has been advanced by Othmar Keel on the basis of iconographic data from the ancient Near East.[2] This rich repository of art and artifacts illuminates many facets of Israelite daily life and clarifies numerous linguistic expressions in Psalms. The following discussion draws on Keel's exten-

---

1. Gustav Hölscher, *Das Buch Hiob*, HAT 17 (Tübingen: Mohr-Siebeck, 1952).
2. Othmar Keel, *The Symbolism of the Biblical World: Ancient Near Eastern Iconography and the Book of Psalms* (Winona Lake, Ind.: Eisenbrauns, 1997).

sive analysis; it is limited to issues for which we have iconographic evidence.

We begin with musical instruments in the ancient Near East. The only two percussion instruments mentioned in Psalms, the cymbal (150:5 only) and tambourine or hand drum (98:6 only), are widely attested elsewhere. Similarly, the wind instruments, trumpet and flute (150:4 only), are often depicted in scenes of festivity. Because of the cost, trumpets appear in royal contexts, whereas a cheaper horn had broader application. It alone was chosen for use in synagogues, in this case a ram's horn, which serves better as a signal of alarm or summons to assemble than as a musical instrument. The stringed instruments, harp (*kinnôr*, thirteen times) and lyre (*nebel*, eight times), differ from one another in that a lyre had a yoke. The lyre could sit on the ground and have as many as ten strings (33:2; 144:9). The lyre's popularity can be seen from its representation on coins associated with Bar Kochbah's revolt as well as from numerous artistic scenes in Egypt and Mesopotamia.

The worshippers assumed a stance of subjection, lying on the ground in *proskynesis* or bowing the knee. Examples of individuals kissing the ground or on one knee illustrate these ways of showing proper respect for deity and expressing a sense of awe. In the view of at least two psalmists, such loyalty belonged solely to Yahweh (81:10; 106:19). Priests enjoyed the special privilege of dwelling in Yahweh's presence; the language of sitting (84:5) and standing (134:1) in the house of the Lord makes this point effectively. The intimacy of this experience in Yahweh's presence finds expression in a beautiful confession: "My eyes are always toward Yahweh" (25:15; 123:1), a concept that underlies several personal names in Ezra and Chronicles. Just as the Persian king sat enthroned on the loyalty of subjects, Yahweh was enthroned on Israel's praises. Trust in the Lord protected worshippers from harm (91); worship of various deities was thought to have provided magical defenses against workers of mischief. A psalmist anticipated help in the morning, the usual occasion for administering justice.

According to Ps 127:1, the successful construction of a house depends on Yahweh's participation. This view accords with ideas of other people concerning the building of temples. The basic understanding of the universe in Psalms resembles that of Israel's neighbors. The center of the world is Babylon in an Akkadian Map of the World, whereas Jerusalem has that central position in Psalms. In popular belief, islands existed alongside the earth disc (97:1; 72:10). Just as other peoples spoke of the divine name filling the earth, psalmists thought of Yahweh's name or glory as doing the same thing. The parallelism of Sea and River in Ugaritic literature occurs in Ps 24:2; 66:6; 80:12. A plurality of heavens (148:4), the heavenly ocean (29:10), and wings as refuge (36:8; 57:2; 61:5; 91:4) correspond to ancient Near Eastern ideology. The Septuagint even translates the divine epithet Rock with *theos,* God.

Creation as a result of conflict between deities representing order and chaos has been widely portrayed. The psalms reflect similar thinking (74:13-17), but Yahweh virtually replaces the dual role of Baal and Yamm, the Ugaritic deities of fertility and drought, life and death. Various representations of a tree of life illustrate the popularity of this notion (cf. Psalm 1), as do depictions of four primordial rivers of paradise. The notion of a city on a hill (87:1) recalls the belief, even in areas of flat land in Egypt such as Medinet Habu, that the sacred temple sits atop a cosmic mountain. The alternative notion that creation resulted from conception and birth plays a small role in Psalms.

Noun lists, or onomastica, resemble the cataloguing of zoological and meteorological phenomena in Psalms 104 and 148, as well as Sirach 43 and Dan 3:29-68 in the Septuagint. The divine abode as a place of impenetrable darkness, a holy of holies, occurs in Egyptian construction of temples with an interior chapel. Various psalms reflect this understanding of Yahweh's dwelling place, but the worshipper also feels the force of such darkness (88:7). In abject misery, one's bones can speak for the person (51:10). Whenever silence prevails in heaven, psalmists detect an absence of Yahweh (94:17).

The frequent language of pits and nets derives from the usual mode of hunting wild animals, but cisterns with no lateral access served as prisons (30). Victory over an enemy was often depicted by showing the conqueror standing with one foot on the defeated person (8:7). The mass slaughter of the vanquished or their enslavement and deportation have inspired a number of paintings, and this harsh reality occurs frequently in Psalms. The transporting of idols to Assur and Babylon and burial of damaged ones demonstrate the seriousness with which statues were taken in the ancient world. This devotion may explain the intense ridicule of idols in Psalms. Dangers at sea are illustrated often, both from stormy seas and from mythical creatures. Psalmists know such obstacles to safe journeys by sea (104:25; cf. Sir 43:24-25).

Numerous scenes illustrate daily worship. The practice of haruspicy may lie behind the spiritualized request in Ps 139:1 that Yahweh examine the worshipper. Priests performed their duties by various means, particularly through haruspicy, the study of the livers of sacrificed animals to determine the future. Gaining a deity's attention occupied the thoughts of many worshippers, some of whom became quite ingenious. As many as 376 ears appear on a stela from Memphis; the ears probably symbolize petition. Departing worshippers received gifts of flowers and fruit as an actualization of priestly blessings (24:5; 67:7; 133:3). Through it all Yahweh functioned as a protective shield. The iconography supports the interpretation of a single shield in Ps 35:2 for the two Hebrew words translated as "shield and buckler"; no soldier wears two protective shields. The psalmist uses the rhetorical feature of hendiadys — two words to convey a single meaning, like law and order — to represent a single shield.

Frequent scenes depict the deity and royal representative as a shepherd, equipped with rod and staff to ward off enemies and protect sheep (23). Psalm 78:70-72 transfers this divine role to David. He also receives a priestly office in Psalm 110; this uniting of royal and priestly roles occurs among Israel's neighbors. The thematization of confidence within Psalms has no parallel in the prayers of other people in the ancient Near East. Even Psalms maintains reserve in depicting divine love, whether paternal or maternal; the same reluctance typifies Egyptians and inhabitants of Mesopotamia. Nevertheless, Yahweh was thought to have formed a child in its mother's womb (139:13, 16).

Despite the strong elevation of royalty in Egypt and Mesopotamia, Israel's prophets mercilessly portrayed the weakness of their own kings. A few psalms refer to Yahweh's adoption of a king and to a royal enthronement (2, 72, 101, 110, perhaps 20 and 21). Divine consecration, blessing, and crowning follow (2:6; 21:6; 45:3). The emphasis on divine generation answered the question, "Why does this person have such power over others?" In Ps 2:7, the temporal "today" indicates the symbolic nature of Yahweh's adoption of the king, for his actual begetting occurred years earlier. Like kings in Egypt and Mesopotamia, Israel's great king, David, was credited with the building of the temple (132:1-5). This ideology persists even when it produces historical inaccuracy: for example, Yahweh's building a temple on Zion and simultaneously choosing David. In Psalms the nations, not chaos, rage against Zion.

Like deities in Egypt and Mesopotamia, Yahweh delivers enemies into the hands of the king (21:8; 110:1), who shatters them (2:8-9). This motif is reversed in an eschatological text (149:8-9); here the kings are bound and executed.

Horses and chariots, frequently represented in royal scenes, gave status to kings. Not everyone believed that victory came from horses (147:8-10; 33:16-17), for Yahweh's will determined the outcome of battles. Two-wheeled chariots, introduced into Syro-Palestine around 1600 BCE, could not easily negotiate the terrain and therefore had more symbolic than real value. The reference to sacrificing rams, goats, and bulls in Ps 66:13-15 probably derives from a royal promise, for ordinary citizens could not afford such a lavish offering. A sense of community resulted when the poor partook of the meals associated with these sacrifices. The mention of tribute from the people of Tyre in Ps 45:2 recalls the wedding between Rameses and the daughter of a Hittite king. Sacred highways led to the city of David (84:6) in the same way they led to temples in neighboring cultures.

The iconographic evidence lends credibility to the claim that the ancient people believed in a multiplicity of approaches toward reality. This conviction enabled them to use concepts that we consider logically contradictory. Truth, as they conceived it, was broader and richer than any single understanding. The same idea could be presented from several perspectives, each of which captured something worth noting. The preponderance of symbolic meanings in this realm of discovery offers a vital clue toward a proper interpretation of biblical imagery. Othmar Keel warns against literalism, noting that the troublesome ending to Psalm 137 ("Happy the one who takes hold of your infants and smashes them on a rock") may be symbolic just like Daughter Babylon in the previous verse (137:8).

FURTHER READING

Keel, Othmar. *The Symbolism of the Biblical World: Ancient Near Eastern Iconography and the Book of Psalms.* Winona Lake, Ind.: Eisenbrauns, 1997.

→ CHAPTER FIVE ←

Classification by Types

Modern study of Psalms owes more to the insights of Hermann Gunkel (1862-1932) than to any other scholar.[1] In studying Psalms, he applied a classification of pure types of literature that had been developed in the wider literary analysis of his day. In this way Gunkel rescued the psalms from the particularity of the historical past and illuminated their typicality. This significant shift enabled him to stress the religious character of the psalms, their importance for daily worship in the present as well as the past.

According to Gunkel, comparison of various psalms yielded five major and seven minor types when one takes into consideration structure, language, and content. The major types, a judgment based on quantity rather than quality, include hymn, lament, individual thanksgiving, and royal psalm. Subcategories exist within hymns, specifically songs of Zion, enthronement psalms, and biblical hymns outside the Psalter. Moreover, laments took two forms, individual and communal. An element of both types of lament, the expression of trust, became a category of its own. The seven minor types consist of pilgrimage psalms, community thanksgiving, wisdom psalms, general liturgies, prophetic liturgies, torah liturgies, and mixed types.

The chief characteristic of hymns is praise of Yahweh, although the reasons for such adulation varied. The origins of the universe and its

---

1. Hermann Gunkel and Joachim Begrich, *An Introduction to the Psalms* (Macon, Ga.: Mercer University Press, 1998 [*Einleitung in die Psalmen,* 1933]).

80

wonders lent themselves to hymnic praise, both within the Bible and among Israel's neighbors. Gunkel's commitment to the "history of religions" approach necessitated comparison on a broader scale than merely within a single culture. Hymns dealing with creation celebrated the generative powers of many different deities; often the same mythic themes occur in hymns separated by hundreds of miles. Biblical hymns also praise Yahweh for the law as instruction for life.

Departing from purely formal criteria, Gunkel identified songs of Zion and enthronement psalms on the basis of subject matter. The centrality of Jerusalem and Yahweh's protection of the divine dwelling place make up the main themes of these songs of Zion. In addition, the songs give voice to pilgrims' longing for Zion and the protection Yahweh offers to loyal subjects. The enthronement psalms reflect divine kingship; the sovereignty of a given deity was a major concern throughout the ancient Near East. Belief in an orderly administration of the world by the deity of a major city or empire was deemed necessary for survival, particularly in preventing a reign of chaos. Hymns praising Yahweh as king over the whole earth often include the subordination of recalcitrant forces. The kingship of God implied power, to be sure, but it also embraced the notion of protection and the administration of justice. Biblical hymns outside the Psalter celebrated national victories like Yahweh's defeat of Pharaoh's army (Exod 15:1-18) and personal moments of triumph (1 Sam 2:1-10).

Communal laments arose when an entire community faced danger so severe that everyone felt the necessity to pray for help. The threat may have been military, the frequent invasion by soldiers from powerful nation-states, particularly Assyria, Babylon, and Persia. Alternatively, potential disasters of other kinds evoked cries for deliverance. Invasions by locusts, persistent drought, devastating fungus on grain, large-scale plagues, earthquakes, and famine — all these threats and more contributed to the sense of helplessness that finds expression in communal laments.

Personal, or individual, laments make up a large part of the Psalter. The occasions of these prayers for help remain relatively obscure, but sickness and slander or a similar personal affront underlie many of them. Gunkel believed that the original circumstances evoking the laments were later generalized to make the prayers more universal. A peculiar feature of laments within Psalms, a decisive transition from plea to confident trust that Yahweh will act to rectify the situation, has even produced a variant psalm type consisting entirely of trust.

These expressions of confidence in Yahweh's disposition to help the person in trouble arose from a history of favorable responses. The resulting thanksgiving psalms by individuals give voice to a deep feeling of appreciation for Yahweh's willingness to act on behalf of the person in difficulty. Stereotypical language hides the precise nature of the dangers that previously overwhelmed the worshipper.

The prominence of kings in the ancient Near East is reflected in the literature that has survived the ravages of time. Gunkel isolates a fifth major type, the royal psalms, from the others and understands it against the backdrop of the Davidic monarchy in Jerusalem. Although few in number, these psalms played a major role in Gunkel's interpretation, for he applied them to the public events involving the reigning descendant of David. Furthermore, he assumed that many other psalms were spoken by the king as representative of the people. The royal psalms celebrated occasions like weddings, coronations, preparation for battle, ritual enactments, and so forth.

The seven minor types indicate a further loosening of firm criteria based on form and language. Pilgrimage psalms, some of which overlap with songs of Zion, allude to a journey to Jerusalem, perhaps a visit during one of the three mandated festivals of the year, and voice a longing to dwell in the holy city. Communal psalms of thanksgiving resemble those attributed to single individuals, except that they express appreciation for deliverance of the entire village, city, or country. Similarities between a few psalms and wisdom literature led Gunkel to include a category of wisdom psalms. These psalms offer advice about succeeding in life, contrast the wise and the wicked, and reflect on life's brevity and human delusion.

Gunkel also paid close attention to liturgical practice in ancient Israel. He noted that some psalms have a change of speaker, that others give voice to prophetic interests, while still others concentrate on the torah. The general liturgies contain elements of the laments, whereas prophetic liturgies have a warning, often in oracular form, by means of which the leader summons the congregation to conduct its life in accordance with Yahweh's will. Torah liturgies focus attention on the conditions for participating in communal worship, the entrance requirements specified in the torah, for which prophetic liturgies also exist. These two liturgies assume alternate voices, that of a prophetic or priestly leader, and those of worshippers.

Even when operating with rather loose criteria, this categorization of the book of Psalms still leaves some of them out. Gunkel groups the remaining psalms in a catch-all category that he labeled "mixed types." He identified Psalms 9–10 as both thanksgiving and lament; similarly, he viewed Psalm 36 as a mixture of lament, hymn, and wisdom. The aforementioned overlap and the resistance to categorization point to the limitation of Gunkel's classification, but by using this approach he almost single-handedly revived the scholarly study of Psalms.

Naturally, subsequent interpreters have made modifications to Gunkel's types, but they have not rejected the basic premise that an appropriate analysis of Psalms begins with classification. Claus Westermann represents a tendency toward simplification.[2] He thinks in terms of two primary types, praise and lament, with two specific kinds of praise, declarative and descriptive. Declarative psalms of praise address the congregation by attesting to Yahweh's deliverance of the people from a given threat, or they describe the specifics of that act on Israel's behalf, and they voice its gratitude. Descriptive praise concentrates on Yahweh's majesty and compassion. The language of creation, sovereign rule, and sustenance sets these psalms apart from the others. Westermann also considers thanksgiving psalms in the same general category as hymns; moreover, psalms of trust could easily fall into this group.

Walter Brueggemann has suggested yet another way of classifying the psalms;[3] he focuses on the effect of individual psalms on readers. Some psalms function as a means of orienting readers to a desirable way of life; other psalms serve to disorient readers, forcing them to question ruling assumptions about thought and action; still other psalms reorient readers by offering a wholly new perspective for viewing reality. Adopting this approach does not preclude the use of other classifications also.

Gunkel's interest in types of psalms was accompanied by a desire to discover the setting in which they functioned. He assumed that

2. Claus Westermann, *Praise and Lament in the Psalms* (Atlanta: John Knox, 1981).

3. Walter Brueggemann, "Psalms and the Life of Faith: A Suggested Typology of Function," *JSOT* 17 (1980): 3-32; and *The Message of the Psalms: A Theological Commentary* (Minneapolis: Augsburg, 1984).

many of them arose in the ordinary events of daily life, particularly Israel at worship. In his view, most of the psalms date from the postexilic period but often reflect earlier piety. Gunkel postulated various occasions for each type of psalm on the basis of Israelite and ancient Near Eastern literature, but his student, Sigmund Mowinckel (1894-1965), pressed the point that the psalms not only originated in worship but were used regularly to add drama to Israel's adoration of Yahweh.[4] Whereas Gunkel noted the significance of emotion, dancing, and singing in Israelite worship, Mowinckel emphasized public ritual, especially ceremonial drama. To him, worship was largely performance, and the cult reinforced both belief and practice, theology and ethics. Mowinckel emphasized the dramatic features within the psalms, including among other things ritual processions, washing of hands, dancing and singing, preparation for sacrifice, waiting at the altar, and public recitation of formative moments in history, especially the Exodus. Refusing to make a radical separation between cult and magic, he believed that evil persons practicing magic lay behind some complaints by worshippers.

Perhaps the most notable concern in Mowinckel's interpretation of Psalms came from anthropological studies. He believed that the king played a central role in Israelite worship, especially during the fall at the annual enthronement festival, to which he ascribed Psalms 47, 95-100. At this event Yahweh's sovereignty over the universe was dramatically presented, with the earthly king as divine representative. In his view, the king spoke many of the laments as representative of the community, but he also embodied the divine life. Mowinckel's approach has been called "cultic actualization," and he made a lasting contribution to a positive understanding of Israel's cultic life. For him, cult was not a late stereotype of an earlier vital piety but the cohesive force uniting worship and life. Together teacher and student shaped the nature of all subsequent interpretation of Psalms. Gunkel pointed to the types and their structures, and Mowinckel emphasized their use in worship. Thanksgiving psalms, for example, may have been brought to the temple in fulfillment of an earlier vow made under duress. Once Yahweh removed the particular affliction, the grateful individual brought a gift to Jerusalem and sang joyfully. Laments may originally have been occa-

---

4. Sigmund Mowinckel, *The Psalms in Israel's Worship* (Nashville: Abingdon, 1962).

sioned by specific threats to life and limb but eventually became generalized to cover almost any danger.

Hymns belonged to the great festivals and to memorable events in national life; in this sense they resembled royal psalms. These celebrations of a Davidic ruler gave the populace an opportunity to participate in royal pageantry. Enthronement psalms, heavenly counterparts to royal psalms, raised the pageantry to a higher realm, acknowledging Yahweh's sovereignty over the gods. These psalms served in the ongoing polemic against idolatry, a struggle that gained new impetus with the fall of Jerusalem and the implication that the gods of Babylon had shown themselves to be more powerful than Yahweh. Similarly, songs of Zion express the people's joy over the physical sign of Yahweh's presence in Jerusalem, the sacred mountain.

Some types of psalms belong to the life of the mind, in Gunkel's view. Wisdom and torah psalms derive from efforts to instruct worshippers in the art of living and in pleasing Yahweh. Prophetic liturgies lend this teaching a serious note, either in the form of a warning or by providing divine oracles. Entrance liturgies, too, guarded against transgression of holy ground by unclean or immoral visitors.

This survey of settings suffers from generalities, but like all modern interpreters, Gunkel was hampered by the limitation of knowledge about daily life in ancient Israel and Judah. Joachim Begrich threw dazzling light on one problem: the surprisingly abrupt change in mood within laments.[5] He proposed that a priest pronounced an oracle to a worshipper, who then gave voice to confidence that Yahweh had heard the prayer and would act to bring healing. Begrich called this word a priestly oracle of salvation; biblical precedent for a priestly oracle exists in Eli's announcement to Hannah that Yahweh had heard her prayer and would give her a son (1 Sam 1:17).

Integral to Gunkel's analysis of different types of psalms was a study of their structure. Lament psalms consisted of invocation, complaint, petition, and conclusion. This analysis calls attention to the logical development of these cries for help. The worshipper invokes Yahweh, describes the misery, begs for mercy, and expresses profound trust. Not every lament has the complete structure, but that flaw in form critical analysis does not negate its utility as a heuristic device.

---

5. Joachim Begrich, "Das priesterliche Heilsorakel," *ZAW* 52 (1934): 81-92.

Structural analysis of hymns yields even fewer positive results; it does little good to know that they consist of introduction, body, and conclusion. Gunkel's keen sense of poetry and appreciation for style, however, go a long way toward compensating for the meager results of analysis into the structure of psalms.

EXCURSUS

Wisdom Psalms

The use of the term "Weisheitsdichtung" (wisdom poetry) in Hermann Gunkel and Joachim Begrich's *Einleitungen in die Psalmen*[1] has produced more confusion than light in the scholarly community. Precisely what the authors meant by wisdom poetry remains unclear, although they specify Psalms 1, 37, 49, 73, 112, and 128 (with parts of 127 and 133 also). To these, Otto Eissfeldt added Psalms 78 and 91, the latter of which quickly faded from discussions of wisdom psalms.[2] Sigmund Mowinckel mentions it in passing, but his enumeration of what he calls "Learned Psalmography" includes 1, 34, 37, 49, 78, 105, 106, 111, 112, and 127.[3] Considerable vacillation on his part makes this list somewhat tenuous.

Despite providing trail-blazing work, both Gunkel and Sigmund Mowinckel subscribed to assumptions that current interpreters no longer accept. Gunkel believed that the forms of psalms evolved from shorter to longer units, and Mowinckel insisted that a didactic psalm is a contradiction in adjective. The texts have not confirmed the form-critical principle that literature developed over time from brief pure forms to more elaborate ones. Likewise the belief that instruction has no place in cultic liturgy appears wrong in principle.

Questioning these earlier authors' fundamental assumptions has not led to a rejection of their conclusions about sapiential psalms. Perhaps a careful examination of later reasons for continuing to speak of such a category will expose the weakness of the case supporting wisdom psalms.

I pass over P. A. Munch and Udo Jansen with a single observation.[4]

---

1. Hermann Gunkel and Joachim Begrich, *An Introduction to the Psalms* (Macon, Ga.: Mercer University Press, 1998 [*Einleitung in die Psalmen*, 1933]), pp. 293-305.

2. Otto Eissfeldt, *The Old Testament: An Introduction* (New York and Evanston: Harper and Row, 1965), p. 125.

3. Sigmund Mowinckel, *The Psalms in Israel's Worship* (Nashville: Abingdon, 1962); and "Psalms and Wisdom," in *Wisdom in Israel and in the Ancient Near East*, VTSup 3 (Leiden: Brill, 1960), pp. 205-24.

4. P. A. Munch, "Die jüdischen 'Weisheitspsalmen' und ihr Platz im Leben," *AcOr*

Munch's distinction between devotional psalms (19B, 25, 119) and instructional psalms (32, 34, and Ps Sol) hardly points to different social settings or traditional lists, and Jansen's comments about similarities between later psalms in Sirach and other deutero-canonical literature and learned psalmography, although largely accurate, obscure a significant time-lapse. At the very least, we must account for the large number of psalms from Mowinckel's list that have found their way into the first two major collections (Books I and II). Leaving the opening psalm aside as a framing supplement, we still have Psalms 34, 37, and 49. For Munch, the point is even more telling; he counts Psalms 19, 25, and 32 in this broader category of learned psalmography.

In this regard, Aage Bentzen shows more caution when limiting wisdom compositions to Psalms 1, 112, and 127.[5] For Bentzen, Psalm 119 falls into a category of its own, a judgment few would dispute given its acrostic uniqueness and its repetitive subjection to ten synonyms for the Hebrew word *tôrāh*. His astute observation that Psalms 32, 37, and 49 belong to thanksgiving psalms echoes Mowinckel on the similar Psalm 73. Unfortunately, Bentzen's important comment that not every psalm on retribution has a didactic function has usually been overlooked by later interpreters.

Roland Murphy's survey of the "state of the discipline" regarding wisdom psalms opts for seven complete psalms (1, 32, 34, 37, 49, 112, and 128), together with brief snippets of sapiential material (25:8-10, 12-14; 31:24-25; 39:5-7; 40:5-6; 62:9-11; 92:7-9; 94:8-15).[6] In defense of this assessment of the evidence, he specifies seven rhetorical devices employed by the sapiential authors: (1) "better than" sayings; (2) numerical sayings; (3) admonition; (4) a teacher's address to sons; (5) the formula of blessing; (6) use of similes; and (7) alphabetic composition. Moving beyond stylistic form to content, Murphy extends his list of criteria for identifying wisdom poems even further to include the juxtaposition of the wicked and the righteous, the notion of two ways, the concept of retribution, the offering of counsel, and the phrase "fear of

---

15 (1937): 112-40; Udo Jansen, *Die spätjüdische Psalmendichtung: Ihr Entstehungskreis und ihr "Sitz im Leben"* (Oslo: Norske videnskaps-akademi, 1937).

5. Aage Bentzen, *Introduction to the Old Testament* (Copenhagen: Gad, 1958), p. 161.

6. Roland Murphy, "A Consideration of the Classification 'Wisdom Psalms,'" in VTSup 9 (Leiden: Brill, 1963), pp. 156-67.

Yahweh." In this context we encounter a significant endeavor to include thanksgiving testimony in didactic discourse.

We can hardly fault Murphy for attempting to support his argument along two lines, for Gunkel also based his judgments on form and content. Nevertheless, this procedure introduces more problems than those inherent to formal analysis of grammar and syntax. Because most psalms cover a broad base theologically and employ highly stereotypical language, the task of identifying the precise subject requires considerable ingenuity and not a little luck. Furthermore, the identification of content, even when correct, merely raises a more pressing issue of social location. Who would have found such a topic worth discussing, a single group or a number of different social entities?

Four of Murphy's five criteria in the realm of content apply also to the prophet Amos as portrayed in the Hebrew Bible. The prophet's social critique of Israelites distinguished between two different groups, the righteous and the wicked. In Amos's view they traveled on different paths, as suggested by his counsel to seek good and not evil as a means of escaping divine retribution. The themes appear frequently in prophetic literature, and this fact militates against equating them with sapiential teachings. These ideas belong rather to a common ideology in the ancient world, one that extended across national boundaries.

The attempt by J. Kenneth Kuntz[7] to move beyond Murphy's findings demonstrates the appropriateness of Norman Whybray's description of the task of identifying wisdom psalms as "making bricks without straw."[8] Kuntz educes evidence of four kinds: (1) rhetorical elements; (2) vocabulary; (3) thematic elements; and (4) forms. On this basis he tries to make a case for nine wisdom psalms, Murphy's seven plus Psalms 127 and 133. The argument, however, has significant flaws, many of which he actually recognizes, without any apparent awareness of how deeply they undercut his thesis.

In discussing the rhetorical elements Kuntz concedes that in no in-

7. J. Kenneth Kuntz, "The Canonical Wisdom Psalms of Ancient Israel — Their Rhetorical, Thematic, and Formal Dimensions," in *Rhetorical Criticism: Essays in Honor of James Muilenburg,* ed. Jared J. Jackson and Martin Kessler (Pittsburgh: Pickwick, 1974), pp. 186-222.

8. Norman Whybray, "The Wisdom Psalms," in *Wisdom in Ancient Israel: Essays in Honour of J. A. Emerton,* ed. John Day, Robert P. Gordon, and H. G. M. Williamson (Cambridge: Cambridge University Press, 1995), pp. 152-60.

stance do all seven occur in a wisdom psalm and that they do not constitute unique stylistic features of the sages. He does not speculate
about the exact number necessary to turn an ordinary psalm into a
sapiential one, nor does he reflect on the implications of shared rhetorical features in ancient Israel. His bold assertion that the formula of
blessing or, better, happiness is an "undeniably crucial wisdom psalms
element" gives the impression of desperation.

Given the minimal results from his examination of the seven rhetorical elements, that moment of near exasperation can be excused. The
"better than" saying appears in Ps 37:16; 63:4; 84:11; 118:8-9; 119:72,
only the first of which Kuntz considers wisdom. Numerical sayings,
too, appear in one wisdom psalm by his count (1:6; the other sayings
are in 27:4; 62:12-13a). Admonitions exist throughout biblical literature and cannot aid Kuntz's cause, and the admonitory address to sons
(34:12) has no parallel in biblical wisdom, which always has the singular "my son." The formula of blessing makes an appearance in six
psalms (1:1; 32:1-2; 34:9; 112:1; 127:5; 128:1), all of which belong to his
list of wisdom psalms. Because this element alone of the seven seems to
bolster his hypothesis, Kuntz labels it crucial. The rhetorical question
(34:13; 49:6) punctuates biblical literature, rendering it useless in isolating wisdom psalms. The same assessment applies to the use of similes in Ps 32:9; 49:15; 128:3, for comparisons belong to the essence of
meaningful discourse. The prophetic literature, for example, abounds
in vivid similes, none of which owes its inspiration to the teaching of
professional sages.

The linguistic basis for attempts to separate sapiential vocabulary
from prophetic, priestly, and everyday discourse appears dubious to
me, for all social groups use language in pretty much the same way, although minor differences in vocabulary and rhetoric may occur here
and there. That reality explains the failure of all efforts to locate vocabulary peculiar to sages. Working on the basis of the seventy-seven words
that R. B. Y. Scott relegated to sapiential use,[9] Kuntz restricts his comments to psalms that have at least nine of the so-called wisdom words.

His remarks become particularly telling in this section. With respect to Psalms 25, 32, 94, 119, and 55 where nine or more words appear, he says, "In this instance, word tabulation is virtually a fruitless

9. R. B. Y. Scott, *The Way of Wisdom* (New York: Macmillan, 1971), pp. 121-22.

effort. . . ."[10] That reaction is not surprising when one considers the other psalms in this category: 1; 5; 19; 25:8-10, 12-14; 37; 49; 73; 92; 139. Two psalms (10 and 107) have ten of Scott's seventy-seven words, but Kuntz considers the findings misleading. Putting aside the actual results that his method produced, Kuntz thinks that only Psalms 1, 32, 37, and 49 qualify as wisdom. Furthermore, he admits, five wisdom psalms have almost none or none at all (34 and 112 have six, 128 has two, 127 has one, and 133 has none).

Seeking additional support for an admittedly weak hypothesis, Kuntz appeals to thematic elements: (1) the fear of Yahweh and veneration of torah; (2) contrasting lifestyles of the righteous and wicked; (3) the reality and inevitability of retribution; and (4) miscellaneous counsels pertaining to daily conduct. Here, too, the results are mixed. Just three psalms refer to the fear of Yahweh (19:10; 34:12; 111:10), and only one of these belongs to wisdom psalms, according to Kuntz. Even this reference to what actually stands for "religion" in the modern sense of the word lacks the identification of fear of Yahweh with its epistemological concomitant, which actually appears in Ps 111:10, a psalm that Kuntz rejects. The full formula should read: piety is the beginning or fundamental principle of learning. Without some such acknowledgment, the mere reference to religion cannot point to a sapiential author.

As for veneration of the torah, the sages prior to Ben Sira used this word in a non-nomistic sense. For them, torah meant parental instruction, teaching based on ancestral tradition rather than Mosaic legislation. By excluding Psalm 119 from his list of sapiential psalms, Kuntz seems to recognize the gulf between veneration of the torah and sapiential teaching.

The other three thematic elements lead Kuntz down a dead-end street, for they were widely shared in ancient Israel. From time immemorial human beings have sharply distinguished between persons acting in socially acceptable ways and others behaving in an unacceptable manner. That inclination to identify behavior worthy of imitating and to disassociate oneself from harmful conduct would probably have been felt across the board, for it represents the drive toward self-protection. Not unexpectedly, the dichotomization of society into opposing groups shows up in literature from quite different social institutions. Such dividing of eth-

10. Kuntz, "The Canonical Wisdom Psalms of Ancient Israel," p. 203.

ical types could point to a particular ideological group, but one would need to show that the criteria for making the selection reflects its peculiar views. Kuntz does not even consider this issue and consequently fails to prove that the classification into good and bad people can be traced to a sage as opposed to a prophet or priest.

These remarks apply even more emphatically to the matter of individual reward and retribution, for the conviction that virtue surpassed vice in achieving well-being penetrated the entire culture. The wise were not the only ones who subscribed to this belief, nor were they alone in suffering when the dogma collapsed, whether temporarily or for the long term. Who would dare to locate the authors of Habakkuk, Genesis 18, Psalm 73, and 2 Esdras in a single camp despite their interest in addressing a singular problem of the human spirit — undeserved and irrational suffering?

The fourth element that Kuntz treats under *theme* has even less evidentiary value. Giving advice about everyday living lies at the heart of legal texts, makes up the warp and woof of prophetic morality, and has a prominent place in priestly exposition. If Kuntz could show that sages offered a unique kind of counsel, one that appears in wisdom psalms but nowhere else outside the sapiential corpus, the argument would carry conviction.

When Kuntz spread the net even wider to cover whole literary types, things simply got out of hand. The decisive issue seems to be quite different from what he thinks. Do the nine psalms in his tabulation of sapiential texts lend themselves to precise categorization? For instance, do the few sentence-proverbs in Psalms 127, 128, and 133 really characterize the entire psalms, or do they merely provide variation to a very different form? Similarly, one can object to Kuntz's selection of acrostic style in Psalms 34 and 37 on the grounds that he excludes other acrostic psalms. Clearly the alphabetic arrangement alone did not provide the clue for him. The last of Kuntz's forms, integrative psalms, gives the appearance of gathering up loose ends.

Perhaps a more exacting analysis of the vocabulary unique to sapiential literature and Psalms would yield more promising results. Avi Hurvitz's exemplary study[11] uncovers only an expression, *sûr mērā*ʿ

---

11. Avi Hurvitz, "Wisdom Vocabulary in the Hebrew Psalter: A Contribution to the Study of 'Wisdom Psalms,'" *VT* 38 (1988): 41-51.

(turn from evil), and a word, *hôn* (wealth). Minimally then, this approach associates four psalms with sapiential discourse (34:15 and 37:27 use "turn from evil"; 112:3 and 119:14 have *hôn*).

The latest investigation of wisdom psalms comes from Norman Whybray,[12] although his primary interest relates to editorial shaping in the Psalter. He designates the following thirteen psalms as pure wisdom: 8, 14 (53), 25, 34, 39, 49, 73, 90, 112, 127, 131, and 139. In addition, Whybray thinks the sages often inserted brief sections into various psalms to give them a sapiential character (18:21-25; 27:11; 32:8-9; 86:11; 92:6-10, 13-15; 94:8-15 [12-13 is secondary]; 105:45; 107:43; 111:2; 144:3-4; 146:3-4). In another context he brings torah psalms (1 and 119) into close relationship with the sapiential ones, for in his words Psalm 1 "sets out like a teacher of wisdom."[13] Whybray writes that Psalms 34, 37, and 78 most resemble wisdom books, that the author of Psalm 49 claims to be a sage, that Psalm 90 and Ecclesiastes have much in common, and that Psalm 73 is a personal confession.

Astonishingly, Whybray manages to come up with almost twice as many wisdom psalms as any other scholar even when rejecting three criteria frequently employed by others: the concept of retribution, the ephemeral character of life, and the formula of blessing. Here he seems to have returned to an earlier abandon that led him to claim that the so-called Succession Narrative owed its inspiration to sages, a position far removed from that which he adopted later when virtually denying the existence of the wise as a professional class.

What prompted him to throw caution to the wind? Whybray became convinced that the decisive criterion for identifying a wisdom psalm was its didacticism. He found precedent in the royal psalms, where content alone sets them apart as a distinct category. Curiously, however, he noted that all liturgical texts have a didactic function, which should have led him either to label the whole Psalter as wisdom or to question his use of this criterion in identifying sapiential psalms.

Three psalms in Whybray's list breathe an air of nationalism (14, 25, 131) or refer to a covenantal relationship between deity and people, neither of which belongs to sapiential discourse before Ben Sira. Four of them (8, 39, 49, 90) reflect on the nature of existence. Deutero-Isaiah's

12. Whybray, "The Wisdom Psalms."
13. Whybray, "The Wisdom Psalms," p. 155.

poetic image of all flesh as grass and the graphic comparison in the Succession Narrative of life as water poured out on the ground demonstrate the ubiquity of reflection on life's essence. Another psalm, 139, concludes the lofty self-examination with a harsh appeal for vengeance paralleled nowhere in wisdom literature, except possibly Ben Sira's outburst against some hated neighbors (Sir 50:25-26). Many of the proverbial glosses may easily have entered the Psalter as prayers of the same people who instructed their children through ancestral tradition.

Erhard Gerstenberger's assumption that the Psalter consists of cultic prayers from synagogal congregations and reflects internal divisions offers a fresh way of looking at this didactic material.[14] He views Psalms 32 and 34 as sapientially inspired, while recognizing wisdom material in 37:2, 8-9, 16, 21. Nevertheless, he believes, the Psalter functioned as a handbook for cultic leaders rather than a guide for private devotion.

My own research in the Psalter leads me to question the very category of wisdom psalms. True, a few psalms treat the same topics that invigorate the author of the book of Job (Psalms 37, 49, and 73) and reflect on life's brevity like Ecclesiastes (39), but these subjects probably exercised the minds of all thoughtful people. I do not see any profit in attributing such psalms to the sages when we know so little about the authors and their social contexts. Perhaps we should limit ourselves to what can definitely be affirmed: some psalms resemble wisdom literature in stressing the importance of learning, struggling to ascertain life's meaning, and employing proverbial lore. Their authorship and provenance matter less than the accuracy and profundity of what they say.

A Listing of Wisdom Psalms

Gunkel/Begrich	1, 37, 49, 73, 112, 128 (91?), Parts of 127 and 133
Eissfeldt	1, 37, 49, 73, 78, 91, 128, 133
Mowinckel	1, 34, 37, 49, 78, 105, 106, 111, 112, 127
Bentzen	1, 112, 127
Murphy	1, 32, 34, 37, 49, 112, 128
	Influence in 25:8-10, 12-14; 31:24-25; 39:5-7; 40:5-6; 62:9-11; 92:7-9; 94:8-15

14. Erhard Gerstenberger, *Psalms: Part I, with an Introduction to Cultic Poetry*, FOTL 14 (Grand Rapids: Eerdmans, 1988).

Kuntz	1, 32, 34, 37, 49, 112, 127, 128, 133
Whybray	8, 14[53], 25, 34, 39, 49, 73, 90, 112, 127, 131, 139
	Glosses in 18:21-25; 27:11; 32:8-9; 86:11; 92:6-15; 94:8-15; 105:45; 107:43; 111:2; 144:3-4; 146:3-4
Hurvitz	*sûr mērā'* in 34:15 and 37:27 and *hôn* in 112:3 and 119:14

FURTHER READING

Anderson, Bernhard W. *Out of the Depths*. Philadelphia: Westminster, 1983; 3rd ed., 2000.

Ballard, H. Wayne, Jr., and W. Dennis Tucker, Jr., eds. *An Introduction to Wisdom Literature and the Psalms*. Macon, Ga.: Mercer University Press, 2000.

Bellinger, W. H. *Psalms: Reading and Studying the Book of Praises*. Peabody: Hendrickson, 1990.

Gerstenberger, Erhard S. *Psalms: Part I, with an Introduction to Cultic Poetry*. FOTL 14. Grand Rapids: Eerdmans, 1988.

Gunkel, Hermann, and Joachim Begrich. *An Introduction to the Psalms*. Macon, Ga.: Mercer University Press, 1998 [*Einleitung in die Psalmen*, 1933].

Levine, Herbert J. *Sing unto God a New Song: A Contemporary Reading of the Psalms*. Bloomington: Indiana University Press, 1995.

Mowinckel, Sigmund. *The Psalms in Israel's Worship*. Nashville: Abingdon, 1962.

Pleins, J. David. *The Psalms: Songs of Tragedy, Hope, and Justice*. Maryknoll: Orbis, 1993.

Sabourin, Leopold. *The Psalms: Their Origin and Meaning*. New York: Abba House, 1974.

Sarna, Nahum M. *Songs of the Heart: An Introduction to the Book of Psalms*. New York: Schocken, 1993.

CHAPTER SIX

Artistic and Theological Design

The Rhetoric of the Psalms

The strong interest in literary features of the Bible over the last quarter of a century has also been reflected in the study of Psalms, where the phenomenon of parallelism has long been recognized. Regardless of the approach an interpreter takes to this echoing feature, whether the traditional differentiation of synonymous, antithetic, and ascending parallelism or a more recent emphasis such as "this particular thing is true and what's more, so is that," the resulting concentration on repetition underscores the power of Hebrew poetry.

Perhaps the poetic device called chiasm has received more attention from interpreters than anything other than parallelism. In this particular pattern, which resembles the letter X, A is followed by B, and the two are then reversed to achieve a sequence of ABB′A′. The possibilities of this scansion seem limitless, for one can apply it on either the macro-level or on the micro-level. Interpreters stress broad concepts like humankind and animal, land and sea, earthly and heavenly, good and bad, gem and flower, and masculine and feminine. They emphasize single letters and words or phrases; moreover, they mark units of greater or lesser scope by means of this feature.

Another poetic device, inclusio, has received considerable attention; in it the demarcation of a unit of poetry or discourse is achieved by using the same word, phrase, or sentence at the beginning and end. In this way a special idea assumes focus and lingers in the subconscious, only to return finally as if to implant itself in the mind permanently. Alphabetic poetry (acrostic), the artificial use of the twenty-two letters of the Hebrew alphabet in proper sequence, also expresses completeness in concept and emotion.

A few psalms make consistent use of a liturgical refrain. Sometimes the refrain actually dominates the whole poetic unit as in Psalm 136, whereas in others such as Psalm 118 it recedes into the background. Occasionally, a refrain seems wholly unified with the poetic unit; an example occurs in Ps 24:8, 10 ("Who is the king of glory?"). The presence of a common refrain in Psalms 42 and 43 aids interpreters in recognizing a single psalm that has been wrongly divided, just as the acrostic principle identifies Psalms 9 and 10 as one poem.

A significant feature of Hebrew poetry, the thematizing of a particular word, has garnered considerable attention. Such thematic words concentrate readers' minds on the essential point in a poem. A notable instance of this thematizing takes place in Psalm 73 where the word "heart" occurs seven times, in this way signifying that the crucial issue under consideration relates to the heart (in its cognitive sense). Purity of heart demands that the worshippers cleanse thoughts that threaten to bring disaster.

Like Hermann Gunkel, interpreters who stress rhetoric also pay close attention to the actual structure of a psalm. They look for features that mark smaller units, search for foreshadowing that spans such indications of demarcation, and specify the signs of reiteration and summation. Critics also look for suasive techniques, metaphorical speech, editorial additions, changes in speakers, direct address to readers, plays on words, and other literary features. This approach, still in its infancy, has enormous potential despite some excesses by its practitioners. The readiness to discover a genius behind ordinary poetry results in too high an appraisal of the literary quality of the psalms. Poetic beauty is certainly there, but much of the book fails to achieve such beauty, and many of the poetic features that excite modern interpreters may either be accidental or mandated by the form itself.

The Shaping of the Psalter

We have already seen rudimentary attempts to arrange the Psalter in a meaningful way, whether on the basis of personal names, liturgical instruction, genre designation, or collections marked off by doxologies. Recent interpreters have pushed this principle further to include ideology and function. This effort, largely subjective, has yielded much discussion but minimal agreement.

The desire to view Psalms in the light of its canonical shape belongs to a perspective advanced by Brevard Childs,[1] who has persisted in this approach to the entire Bible despite harsh criticism from several scholars. The antagonism was generated partly by the manner in which Childs dismisses previous scholarship by historical critics in favor of insights from the Reformation, especially Calvin, but also by the arbitrary decision to rely wholly on the final form of the Hebrew Bible rather than the Septuagint or other ancient texts such as those from Qumran.

The initial impetus to the study of design in Psalms came from Gerald Wilson,[2] who sought to demonstrate that the Psalter depicts the bankruptcy of the Davidic monarchy and its replacement by Yahweh as king. The evidence for this view consists largely of influences from the positioning of psalms about a human king within the five major divisions. In Book I the powerful endorsement of the Davidic ruler stands at the very beginning after the introductory psalm to the entire Psalter, but in Books II and III royal psalms appear at the end. Thus Psalm 2 identifies the king as Yahweh's adopted son, the anointed one in Zion, and promises that mastery of the nations is his for the asking. The divine recognition of kingship in Psalm 2 gives way to human supplication on the king's behalf in Psalm 72. The people pray that the king will implement justice, bring prosperity, extend his kingdom, and reach a happy old age.

In Psalm 89 the speaker recalls Yahweh's promise to David and extols divine integrity before conceding that the one who cannot lie has nevertheless removed the scepter from David's house. The psalm closes

1. Brevard S. Childs, "Reflections on the Modern Study of the Psalms," in *Magnalia Dei: The Mighty Acts of God*, ed. F. M. Cross et al. (Garden City, N.Y.: Doubleday, 1976), pp. 377-88.

2. Gerald H. Wilson, *The Editing of the Hebrew Psalter* (Chico, Calif.: Scholars Press, 1985).

with a poignant question: "Lord, where is your former steadfast love? You swore to David by your faithfulness" (v. 50). Bracketing this query is a twofold appeal for remembrance and a formulaic "How long, Yahweh, will you conceal yourself forever; will your anger burn like fire?" (vv. 47, 48, 51).

Books IV and V, according to this hypothesis, depict Yahweh as Israel's true monarch. Furthermore, Book V transfers to the people the royal claims of the Davidic family. According to Wilson, Book IV explores the implications of the demise of Davidic kingship, and Book V offers hope through the divine ruler. Psalm 1 furnishes the hermeneutical perspective that leads Wilson to search for the seams in the larger work. He relies on various clues, however, especially the attribution of particular psalms to authors, the superscriptions that point to intentional arrangement, implicit evidence such as the juxtaposition of titled and untitled psalms, certain phrases, doxologies, and the grouping of hallelujah psalms at the end.

Clinton McCann offers a variant of Wilson's interpretation;[3] he understands Psalm 2 in light of a tradition in the Bible that recognizes Yahweh as true king even when human rulers occupy the throne in Jerusalem. In Psalm 2 the emphasis falls on Yahweh, not on his anointed, and this position, reaffirmed in Psalms 72 and 89, is reinforced in Psalms 93, 95-99. The shout, "Yahweh has become king" or "Yahweh reigns," resounds through the latter group of psalms, together with an observation about justice and might.

For McCann, Psalm 73 constitutes the theological transition of the Psalter, a microcosm of Old Testament theology, and Book IV is the theological heart of Psalms. The shift in Psalm 73 from doubt to trust, made possible by attendance at the divine sanctuary, marks a highpoint, to be sure, but earlier psalms attain similar pinnacles, and psalms subsequent to 73 return to feelings of abandonment by Yahweh. Moreover, the sharp disagreement among interpreters over what constitutes the central feature of biblical theology reveals the precarious nature of all claims about theological centers.

An alternative to these hypotheses focusing on kingship has come

---

3. J. Clinton McCann, "Psalms," in *NIB*, vol. IV (Nashville: Abingdon, 1996), pp. 741-1280; and "Psalm 73: A Microcosm of Old Testament Theology," in *The Listening Heart* (Sheffield: JSOT, 1987), pp. 247-57.

from James Mays,[4] who views the three torah psalms as the key to the final form of the Psalter. His thesis resembles to some extent that of Claus Westermann,[5] who claimed that Psalms 1 and 119 introduce and conclude an original book of Psalms, to which editors have added subsequent materials. For both scholars, Psalm 1 shapes the Psalter as devotional reading, or better still, meditation. Psalm 119 may illustrate the possibilities inherent to such an approach to torah, but it seems doubtful that this kind of meditation has anything to do with the Psalter itself. The same observation applies to Psalm 1, which encourages readers and auditors to reflect on Yahweh's torah. Arguably, this noun carries the specific nuance of the Pentateuch, although torah often has a much broader meaning that could extend as far as the context of the Psalter. Nevertheless, that interpretation of torah ignores the explicit designation of Psalms as human prayers and expressions of praise. Such words from below, as it were, may point others in the direction they should go, hence function as torah, but they differ appreciably from divine oracles and legislation. Neither Childs nor Westermann seems to be bothered by this problem. For them, the Psalter comprises a manual of piety with law at the center. Prayer has therefore been transformed into Yahweh's word for all people.

The process by which this transformation took place can be viewed in Ps 19:8-15, according to Hans-Joachim Kraus, whose commentary and theological analysis of the Psalter set the standard for contemporary analysis.[6] In his view, this section of Psalm 19 decodes the inaudible speech of verses 1-7 in light of the torah. In this way, a Canaanite hymn becomes thoroughly Yahwistic; such absorption of Canaanite material is a familiar practice in the Old Testament. Not everyone agrees, however, that the old hymn derives from Canaanite worship; Odil Hannes Steck[7] and Peter Craigie[8] locate its origin in what they take to be wisdom discourse, particularly Genesis 1–3.

---

4. James Mays, "The Place of the Torah-Psalms in the Psalter," *JBL* 106 (1987): 3-12.

5. Claus Westermann, *Praise and Lament in the Psalms* (Atlanta: John Knox, 1981).

6. Hans-Joachim Kraus, *Psalms 1–59* (Minneapolis: Augsburg, 1988); and *Psalms 60–150* (Minneapolis: Augsburg, 1989).

7. Odil Hannes Steck, "Bemerkungen zur thematische Einheit von Psalm 19,2-7," in *Werden und Wirken des Alten Testaments: Festschrift für Claus Westermann zum 70. Geburtstag,* ed. Reiner Albertz et al. (Göttingen: Vandenhoeck & Ruprecht, 1980), pp. 318-24.

8. Peter Craigie, *Psalms 1–50* (Waco: Word, 1983).

Several interpreters have argued that one can detect a definite movement in Psalms from lament to praise. Undoubtedly, the final five psalms offer resounding praise to Yahweh, but a straight movement away from lament does not occur in Books IV and V. One can speak of a general increase in praise toward the end of the Psalter, but too many exceptions rule out the conclusion enunciated above with regard to the suppression of lament by exuberant praise.

Yet another attempt to discern intentional shaping in the Psalter takes its cue from the overt interest in liturgy, both in the super-scriptions and in the psalms themselves. Carroll Stuhlmueller discerns a movement from ordinary to liturgical language as one progresses toward the end of Psalms.[9] He detects a new attention to liturgy in Book III, concluding in Book V with the most liturgical psalms of all. The latter includes a collection of psalms focusing on the three major festivals in ancient Israel (113-118) and a booklet for pilgrims (120-134).

Stuhlmueller calls attention to a comparable shift in terminology from what he considers a more secular word for blessing (*'ašrē*, "happy") in Psalm 1 to the "sacred" verb *bārak* (to bless), which appears three times in Psalm 134. Here, too, the Psalter offers evidence that places the theory in jeopardy; the presence of a liturgical text in Psalm 24 seems strangely out of place for the hypothesis, in its extreme form. In general, however, the argument has merit.

An alternative to the shaping of the Psalter through attention to kingship or liturgical interest has come from J. Reindl[10] and Norman Whybray,[11] who believe that editors from wisdom circles have intentionally inserted brief verses representing their own views. The presence of what Sigmund Mowinckel called learned psalmography has long been recognized, but the several attempts to explain this material have been less than satisfactory. Gunkel thought that only the torah and wisdom psalms in the Psalter originated outside the official cult and

9. Carroll Stuhlmueller, "Psalms," in *Harper's Bible Commentary* (San Francisco: Harper and Row, 1988), pp. 433-94.

10. J. Reindl, "Weisheitliche Bearbeitung von Psalmen: Ein Beitrag zum Verständnis der Sammlung des Psalters," in *Congress Volume, Vienna 1980*, VTSup 32 (Leiden: Brill, 1981), pp. 333-54.

11. Norman Whybray, *Reading the Psalms as a Book*, JSOTSS 222 (Sheffield: Sheffield Academic Press, 1996).

were added as a result of pressure on priests from the laity. This material defies classification because of a mixture of forms typical of late psalmography, according to both Gunkel and Mowinckel, the latter of whom postulated a school for scribes within the temple, the original location for the composition of these psalms. In Mowinckel's view, these scribes collected and edited the entire Psalter, adding their own special compositions. Along these lines Udo Jansen argued that this scribal school trained courtiers, as well as legal scribes like Ben Sira, but both the existence of such schools and the accuracy of designating Ben Sira as a legal scribe have been questioned.

The initial challenge to the dominant view that temple singers composed the Psalter came from Reindl, who located the wisdom compilers in the second temple and envisioned them as Ben Sira's predecessors. In his view, Psalm 1 addressed students in this school by showing them the correct mode of behavior as dictated by Yahweh. Reindl sought to illustrate the complicated process by which these editors altered traditional psalms and transformed them into safe advice. For example, they added minor snippets like the following: "But to the wicked God says" (50:16), "Let sinners be destroyed from the earth and the wicked vanish" (104:35), and "but (Yahweh) ruins the way of the wicked" (146:9b). The scribes also juxtaposed particular psalms such as 105 and 106, 111 and 112, and 90–92 in an effort to influence the way they would be understood. In addition, according to Reindl, the editors provided links between verses to make the total composition more compatible with their own views.

The alignment of Psalms 105 and 106 makes it necessary to view the memorable events associated with the Exodus from completely different perspectives. The poet of the first remembers only the positive features of that experience, whereas the second psalm forces readers and hearers to reflect on the people's rebellious character. The bright mood of Psalm 105 quickly dissipates into a somber one in the next psalm. By placing Psalm 112 directly after the concluding verse in Psalm 111, a motto from wisdom literature ("The fear of Yahweh is the beginning [or first principle] of wisdom," 111:10a, with inverted phrasing to meet the requirement of the acrostic poem) leads into a pronouncement that anyone who fears Yahweh is happy. The two psalms have stylistic symmetry, for each one uses a rare acrostic form that applies to half verses. Elsewhere the acrostics in the Psalter work on the basis of an entire verse (25, 34, 145), two verses (9–10, 37) and eight verses (119).

Whybray develops this idea of editorial glosses within the Psalter much further, including the addition of both torah and wisdom psalms. He views Ps 19:8-15 as a supplement that transforms an old hymn into an inducement to observe the torah. Similarly, he thinks verses 30-31 give Psalm 37, a didactic poem about the principle of retribution, a distinct turn toward the torah. Another gloss in Ps 40:7-9 accomplishes the same thing, but in more graphic language.

> Sacrifice and offering you take no delight in,
> You have opened my ears;
> Burnt offering and sin offering you have not demanded.
> Then I said, "Behold, I have come;
> In the scroll of the writing is written concerning me;
> To do your pleasure, my God, I am pleased,
> And your torah lodges deep within me."

By adding verses 5-8, 10 to Psalm 78, the editors changed a wisdom psalm into one with a distinct interest in torah. The possibilities of this approach appear limitless, and Whybray proceeds relentlessly in isolating supposed glosses.

Moving on to interpolation of wisdom materials, he finds additions in Ps 18:21-25; 27:11; 32:8-9; 86:11; 92:7-8 [6-10], 13-15; 94:8-15 (8-11, 12-13 is secondary); 105:45; 107:43; 111:2; 144:3-4; 146:3-4. The ending of Psalm 107 ("Whoever is wise, let him observe these things; and let them consider Yahweh's compassionate deeds") resembles the conclusion to Hosea (14:10a), although the cognitive language of the latter gloss ("understand," "discerning," "know") sounds more authentically wisdom to some interpreters. Here we come face to face with the problem of identifying specific vocabulary and ideas of the sages. Another fly in the ointment renders the approach problematic: what objective criteria exist for recognizing glosses in the psalms? Without syntactic disjuncture, and with little agreement over what constitutes wisdom language and ideology, the hypothesis stands or falls with the careful evaluation of each supposed gloss.

The affirmation of a principle of reward and retribution in Ps 18:21-25 hardly stands out as distinctive of Israelite wisdom, for the entire society subscribed to this belief and complained openly when Yahweh seemed to have overlooked it. The teacher's observation in Ps 32:8-9 could easily be a divine oracle like the unforgettable word in Isa 30:20-21 from the matchless teacher, no longer hidden but eager to prevent any misstep (". . . This is the way; walk in it"). The appeal in Ps 32:9 to the behavior of domestic animals, certainly present in wisdom literature, does not settle the issue, for prophets also used such arguments. The request in Ps 27:11 that Yahweh perform the role of teacher when parents abandon this responsibility shows that a psalmist could speak of Yahweh as teacher. The prayer in Ps 86:11 therefore conforms to the usual piety in the Psalter; nothing in this verse points to distinctive ideas in wisdom literature.

Although the author of Ecclesiastes reflects on the profundity and elusiveness of wisdom (Eccles 7:23-29), that argument differs from the psalmist's concession that Yahweh's thoughts are exceedingly profound (92:6). To be sure, the following verse underscores mental dullness, but the real point of verses 7-8 seems to relate to punishment for wrongdoing, not intellectual adroitness. The final two verses merely direct attention to the reverse side of the coin, the prosperity of the righteous; they therefore support the dogma of divine justice.

One feature of Ps 94:8-11 coincides with an interest in wisdom literature, specifically Ecclesiastes' dismissing of human thoughts as ephemeral; but the emphasis on disciplining nations departs from the fundamental individualism of the wise. By no stretch of the imagination can Ps 106:45 derive from a sage, for the allocation of land to a chosen nation for the purpose of observing Yahweh's statutes sounds more like Deuteronomy than Proverbs, Job, and Ecclesiastes. Even less persuasive is the attribution of Ps 111:2 to the wise ("Great are Yahweh's works, sought out for all their delights").

The last two texts that Whybray considered glosses by an editor steeped in wisdom categorize human existence, focusing on life's transitory nature. The idea in Ps 144:3-4 reiterates a sentiment also found in Psalm 8: Yahweh's taking notice of mortals defies all understanding. The comparison of life to a breath and to a shadow echoes certain parts of the book of Ecclesiastes, but the symbolism probably occurred to anyone who thought seriously about the problem. Mortals return to the earth after drawing their last breath (146:3-4); that belief goes back to Israel's myth of human beginnings.

Whybray's next move is bolder still. He extends the scope of wisdom psalms to thirteen, or more correctly twelve, for Psalm 53 replicates 14 (8; 14; 53; 25; 34; 39; 49; 73; 90; 112; 127; 131; 139). The disagreement among scholars on this much-discussed category seems to grow wider with each participant in the debate. The situation is not likely to change in the foreseeable future.

FURTHER READING

Childs, Brevard S. "Reflections on the Modern Study of the Psalms." In *Magnalia Dei: The Mighty Acts of God*, ed. F. M. Cross et al., pp. 377-88. Garden City, N.Y.: Doubleday, 1976.

Creach, Jerome F. D. *Yahweh as Refuge and the Editing of the Hebrew Psalter.* JSOTSS 217. Sheffield: Sheffield Academic Press, 1996.

de Claissé-Walford, Nancy. *Reading from the Beginning: The Shaping of the Hebrew Psalter.* Macon, Ga.: Mercer University Press, 1997.

Howard, David M., Jr. "Psalm 94 among the Kingship of Yhwh Psalms." *CBQ* 61 (1999): 667-85.

———. *The Structure of Psalms 93–100.* Biblical and Judaic Studies, vol 5. Winona Lake, Ind.: Eisenbrauns, 1997.

Interpretation 46.2 (1992 — The Book of Psalms).

McCann, J. Clinton, ed. *The Shape and Shaping of the Psalter.* JSOTSS 159. Sheffield: JSOT, 1993.

Whybray, R. Norman. *Reading the Psalms as a Book.* JSOTSS 222. Sheffield: Sheffield Academic Press, 1996.

Wilson, Gerald H. *The Editing of the Hebrew Psalter.* SBLDS 76. Chico, Calif.: Scholars Press, 1985.

✦ PART III ✦

SOME READINGS

CHAPTER SEVEN

Standing near the Flame: Psalm 73

1 Truly, El is good to the upright,
   Elohim to those whose hearts are pure.
2 But as for me, my feet almost stumbled,
   my steps nearly slipped.
3 For I envied the arrogant
   when I saw the well-being of the wicked.
4 For they have no pangs;
   their bodies are whole and well nourished.
5 They do not experience trouble like ordinary people,
   and are not smitten along with other humans.
6 Therefore pride is their necklace;
   violence covers them like a garment.
7 Their eyes proceed from abundance;
   wild imaginations pass through their minds.
8 They descend into the depth and speak malice;
   from on high they declare oppression.
9 They place their mouth in heaven,
   and their tongue walks on earth.
10 Therefore the people return hither
    and sip abundant waters for themselves.

The material in this chapter appeared previously in James L. Crenshaw, *A Whirlpool of Torment: Israelite Traditions of God as an Oppressive Presence* (Philadelphia: Fortress, 1984), pp. 93-108.

11 They say, "How can God know?
   Is there knowledge in the Most High?"
12 Lo, these are the sinners;
   ever at ease, they amass a fortune.
13 Entirely in vain have I cleansed my heart
   and washed my hands in innocence.
14 For I suffer torment throughout the day,
   am chastened in the morning.
15 If I had dared to say, "I shall proclaim such things,"
   I would have betrayed the generation of your children.
16 But when I pondered the way to understand this,
   it was burdensome in my sight
17 Until I went into the sanctuary of God,
   [and] I understood their fate.
18 Truly you set them in slippery places;
   you make them fall to deceptions.
19 How quickly they are destroyed;
   they are utterly swept away by calamity.
20 Like a dream when the Lord awakes;
   on awakening, you despise their phantoms.
21 When my heart was embittered,
   and my inner being was pierced,
22 I was stupid and unknowing;
   I was like Behemoth before you.
23 But I am continually with you;
   you hold me by my right hand.
24 You lead me by your counsel,
   and afterward you receive me [in] honor.
25 Whom have I in heaven [but you],
   and besides you I desire nothing on earth.
26 My flesh and my heart may waste away;
   God is my rock and portion forever.
27 For those far away from you will perish;
   you will silence all those who betray you.
28 But as for me, God's drawing near is good to me;
   I have made the Lord God my refuge,
      to proclaim all your works.

Some things are best communicated by personal testimony. This is particularly true of those instances where God's goodness stands in jeopardy because of a world that seems crooked. In a proper universe, good deeds receive their just rewards and wicked conduct is promptly punished. Such is the unreal world that persons of deep religious convictions have painted for millennia. The survival of that vision of a just world order has come only at enormous expense. Psalm 73 tells the story of one such instance when religious claims clashed with stark reality and almost destroyed a believer.[1]

The Structure

In the psalm the spotlight shifts back and forth from the anguished believer to the irreligious throng that is the occasion for doubt about God's justice. This alternating focus is achieved as well within the framework of the psalm, the first three verses and the last two. In the initial verses the psalmist is in danger of slipping into the camp of those who credit God with ignorance. At the end this lonely figure has planted both feet firmly on the rock that none can move. Far away in the distant regions the crowd of sinners who prospered in the beginning now fades into nothingness.

Sandwiched between these two descriptions of a single believer and numerous detractors is an account of a faith that was sorely tested. This story consists of envious reporting on the life-style of the wicked (vv. 4-12) and the resulting temptation to become like them (vv. 13-16). Yet the psalmist's confession does not stop there; instead it proclaims a turning point in the sanctuary of God (v. 17) that threw fresh light on

---

1. Martin Buber's exposition of Psalm 73 penetrates to the heart of the problem and is therefore indispensable for anyone who wishes to understand its pathos ("The Heart Determines [Psalm 73]," in *On the Bible* [New York: Schocken Books, 1968], pp. 199-210). J. Luyten ("Psalm 73 and Wisdom," in *La Sagesse de l'Ancien Testament,* ed. Maurice Gilbert [Gembloux: Editions J. Duculot; Leuven: University Press, 1979], pp. 59-81) views this psalm from the perspective of sapiential literature, as does Leo G. Perdue (*Wisdom and Cult,* SBLDS 30 [Missoula, Mont.: Scholars Press, 1977], pp. 286-91). However, James F. Ross ("Psalm 73," in *Israelite Wisdom,* ed. J. G. Gammie et al. [Missoula, Mont.: Scholars Press, 1978], pp. 161-75) prefers to emphasize "both-and." For him the psalm is related to wisdom and to Psalms in general (lament, trust, and thanksgiving).

the fate of the wicked (vv. 18-20) and gave birth to renewed trust in divine goodness (vv. 21-26).

The Theme

The first verse announces the theme of the psalm. It is stated in the form of a creed: "Truly God is good to Israel, to those whose hearts are pure." We recognize at once that something is awkward, to say the least. The verse seems to suggest that all Israelites possess pure hearts, for the synonymous parallelism certainly implies that. For this reason many interpreters divide the Hebrew letters differently, reading *layyāšār 'ēl*[2] instead of *lᵉyiśrā'ēl* and translating as follows: "Truly El (God) is good to the upright, Elohim to the pure in heart."

The psalm illustrates the manner in which religious convictions undergo radical testing and important reformulation. The final expression of the theme differs considerably from its original form. The weighty experiences that the psalmist reflects on have transformed the meaning of divine goodness. Faith has matured in the process. At first the emphasis fell on gifts that the deity dispensed like Santa Claus to all those who have been good. The ultimate understanding of divine goodness soars to new spiritual heights. From this lofty perch the psalmist understands that the supreme good is the privilege of being near God.

The Setting

The psalmist has taken an individual personal experience and fashioned it into a typical one with universal applicability. What that lone individual experienced was true to life. Others could readily identify with the author, for the test of faith was no isolated case. We look in vain for some specific clues about the psalmist's identity. Who was the author, and what were the historical circumstances that shaped human destiny as we see it unfold before our very eyes?

2. "God to the upright." If, however, Israel is retained, one may contrast divine justice to the nation with a sense of injustice on the individual level. That does not seem to be the emphasis in this psalm, although a sense of individual worth may have been heightened during the time of the psalm's composition.

Scholars have tried to reconstruct the situation by reading between the lines in v. 17 ("until I went to God's sanctuary [and] perceived their fate"). For some this brief allusion to a holy place suggests that the psalm belongs to the repertoire of the cult.[3] The thesis has even been altered to include the claim of royal authorship, largely because of an assumed echo in v. 23 of an Egyptian ritual during which the deity grasped the pharaoh by the right hand.[4] Perhaps it is significant that Psalm 73 begins the third book of the Psalter.[5] In the eyes of the person responsible for the headings in the Psalms, King David's prayers came to an end with Psalm 72. Book III begins with a group of psalms that is attributed to Asaph.[6] This attribution of Psalm 73 to Asaph does nothing to encourage a royal interpretation.

Is there another way to reach an approximate date and setting for this psalm? The usual procedure — that is, the attempt to place various psalms on a continuum according to their theological perspective[7] — runs the risk of circular reasoning and should therefore be used with caution. Naturally, this approach assumes that religious ideas progressed ever more in ancient Israel, and the purest teachings necessarily came later than others less refined. Of course, we know that societies do not evolve in this fashion, and pockets of a culture invariably preserve older values, just as the Rechabites, those intrepid preservers of the tent-dweller's way of life, did in the biblical world.

---

3. Ernst Würthwein, "Erwägungen zu Ps 73," in *Wort and Existenz: Studien zum Alten Testament* (Göttingen: Vandenhoeck & Ruprecht, 1970), pp. 161-78, originally in *Festschrift für A. Bertholet* (Tübingen: J. C. B. Mohr [Paul Siebeck], 1950), pp. 532-49; Helmer Ringgren, "Einige Bemerkungen zum 73. Psalm," *VT* 3 (1953): 265-72.

4. Würthwein ("Erwägungen zu Ps 73," p. 171) refers to Hugo Gressmann's belief that the reference echoes the Babylonian New Year ritual in which a god takes the reigning king by the right hand.

5. The five divisions are Pss 1-41, 42-72, 73-89, 90-106, 107-50.

6. Michael D. Goulder (*The Psalms of Asaph and the Pentateuch,* JSOT SS 233 [Sheffield: Sheffield Academic Press, 1996]) probes the context in which these psalms are placed in search of clues as to their origin and function. He thinks they are a liturgy of a national festival of the Danite sanctuary.

7. The interpretation of the Old Testament has been plagued by this necessity to argue from the development of religious thought to history and from historical context to the date of the literature. For this reason, all judgments about the relative dates of biblical texts are hazardous.

The Religious Problem

Nevertheless, certain psalms do belong together because of the similarities in the religious problems they examine. These are Psalms 37, 49,
and 73.[8] In the first of these the mood is a triumphant one. There is really no theological problem, and believers are encouraged to refrain
from worry over the apparent prosperity of the wicked, who will soon
perish. The author of Psalm 37 has lived for many years and comes forward to testify that no instance of the righteous going hungry has ever
darkened his sight. Psalm 49 also recognizes death as the destiny of sinners, whose wealth fails them in that hour. The believer fares much
better, for God ransoms the soul of the psalmist from Sheol. Death,
shepherd of sinners, will herd them into the realm of shadows.[9]

At which end of the spectrum does Psalm 73 occupy a place? Does
the author represent an early stage in religious experience that has yet to
achieve the assurance manifesting itself in the other two psalms? Or does
Psalm 73 represent a late breakthrough in spirituality? Those are the
questions we cannot answer with confidence. It follows that we shall of
necessity leave many issues about the setting of the psalm unresolved.

One thing is clear beyond the slightest doubt. The theological
problem addressed in all three psalms is what we have learned to call a
theodicy.[10] How can one justify God's ways in the face of apparent evidence to the contrary? Psalm 73 achieves fresh insight into the resolu-
tion of this vexing problem. It suggests that the issue has been stated
falsely, and therefore the author restates the problem. In essence the
psalmist contends that the goods of this world are wholly irrelevant to
the matter of God's justice. Proof of God's goodness rests in divine
presence, not in material prosperity.

---

8. Commentators generally discuss these three psalms together because of the simi-
larity in subject, e.g., Hans-Joachim Kraus, *Theologie der Psalmen*, BKAT 15 (Neukirchen-
Vluyn: Neukirchener Verlag, 1979), p. 212.

9. Leo Perdue, "The Riddles of Psalm 49," *JBL* 93 (1974): 533-42.

10. Kraus (*Theologie der Psalmen*, p. 212) observes that Psalms 49 and 73 do not raise
the *general* issue of theodicy but the *particular* problem: Why must God's servant suffer?
It is typical for Israelite thinkers to reflect on concrete problems rather than on the ab-
stract issue itself. Nevertheless, occasionally they did even speculate about the nature of
God, the divine essence. See Ludwig Schmidt, *"De Deo,"* BZAW 143 (Berlin and New
York: Walter de Gruyter, 1976).

Such an unorthodox solution flew in the face of traditional teaching. For generations the wisest of Israel's teachers had found evidence of God's approval in long life, wealth, and reputation. One need not look for long within the pages of the Hebrew Bible to discover traces of this affirmation. It motivated some of Israel's noblest leaders and sustained them in difficult times. In an important sense the conviction that the deity ruled over a just universe enabled decent human beings to believe that their conduct held the fabric of the world together. Therefore they could hardly be accused of acting solely out of self-interest.[11]

Why then did the author of Psalm 73 reject this traditional view? Surely others recognized the difficulty of proving God's goodness when corruption ruled the day. Yet they found the moral courage to affirm the incredible and thus transmitted the tradition despite evidence to the contrary. We shall seek an answer to this question by examining the psalm in more detail.

Key Concept: Heart

We turn first to consider the key concept in Psalm 73, the word "heart,"[12] which occurs six times in this short psalm (vv. 1, 7, 13, 21, 26 [2]). Perhaps we ought to delete the second use in v. 26, for the resulting sentence is actually an improvement over the present text. We would then translate the verse "My flesh and my heart may waste away; God is my rock and portion for ever."[13]

The word "heart" dominates the vocabulary precisely because the state of the heart, that is, the center of the intellect, is at stake. A pure heart beats its lonely drum while impure hearts set up a deafening noise that functions to draw outsiders toward its vitality. The crisis oc-

---

11. This insight arose largely from study of Egyptian wisdom, for it soon became apparent that conduct that upheld *maat* (justice, order) could hardly be considered self-centered, although it did bring well-being to the individual. Proper behavior sustained the universe and was thus in accord with divine will (H. H. Schmid, *Wesen and Geschichte der Weisheit*, BZAW 101 [Berlin: Alfred Töpelmann, 1966]; and *Gerechtigkeit als Weltordnung*, BHT 40 [Tübingen: J. C. B. Mohr (Paul Siebeck), 1968]).

12. Buber, "The Heart Determines (Psalm 73)," p. 201.

13. This choice of the easier text violates the principle of textual criticism that the most difficult text is preferable.

curs when the psalmist questions the wisdom of keeping the heart pure and hands clean. Nevertheless, this attitude does not prevail, for the author understands how perilously close to brutish behavior these thoughts have led. The inner being has secretly envied the wicked, and this awareness comes as a bitter revelation. In the final analysis, the psalmist realizes that the fragile heart may fail, although its purity is beyond question. Therefore the eyes penetrate the darkness in search of a permanent refuge. They soon come to rest on the rock of ages.

The heart is not the only part of the body that the psalmist endeavors to purify. The hands also retain their innocence, although the author imagines that their ritual cleanliness is in vain (v. 13). It is significant that God reaches out and takes hold of the psalmist's right hand as if to assure the surprised believer of continued divine presence (v. 23).

Indeed, the entire psalm is rich in allusions to parts of the body, as if to draw the reader's attention to the central force of the words "heart" and "hand." The psalmist's feet have almost stumbled; the eyes of the sinners swell with fatness, and these wicked persons set their mouths against the heavens while their tongue struts through the earth; the psalmist's inner parts were poignantly pierced, and the outer flesh will eventually waste away. The final breakthrough may transcend the physical, but the psalm does not gloss over the important fact that we are creatures who feel and touch and see. That down-to-earth quality is in no small measure the explanation for the extraordinary power Psalm 73 wields within the community of faith.

Yet another feature of the language in this psalm strikes the reader as unusual: the threefold use of the intensifying adverb 'ak, "truly" (vv. 1, 13, 18). Such an exclamation is at home in the world of affirmation. It functions like a creed; this I believe beyond the shadow of a doubt. Nevertheless, the exclamation occurs in three distinct contexts. The first is the motto that has suddenly come into question; it concerns the issue of divine goodness toward the pure in heart. The second is the false assertion that the psalmist's innocence is wholly without value. The last use of the exclamation gives voice to the conviction that the deity causes the wicked to slip and to fall into oblivion. This assurance underscores the correctness of the original claim that God is good to the pure in heart, since punishment of the wicked belongs to the underside of belief in divine goodness.

One could even say that two creedal statements occur here, one positive and the other negative. By their very nature these assertions focus on divine activity. Between these two confessions about the Lord lies one about the psalmist that registers sinister thoughts: "Entirely in vain have I cleansed my heart and washed my hands in innocence" (v. 13). Although the unthinkable had forced itself on the mind of the troubled author, such negative thoughts did not triumph in the end. What prevented capitulation to these seductive forces? In a word, loyalty to the people of God (v. 15).

Have we thus stumbled on a clue that would assist in answering the question posed earlier: Why did the psalmist abandon tradition? Personal integrity prevented this sensitive believer from proclaiming anything that might cause the generation of God's children to go astray, if that is the sense of the Hebrew. Alternatively, this integrity did not allow betrayal of God's family, that is, the psalmist refused to *deny* the fundamental tenets passed on from one generation to another. Instead, this true child of faith groped in the darkness for a means of affirming traditional views while simultaneously raising the discussion to another level. For such a one, purity of heart was no small matter. Surely this personal story will reward closer analysis.

Psalm 73

The Frame (73:1-3, 27-28)

<blockquote>
¹ Truly El is good to the upright,
  Elohim to those whose hearts are pure.
² But as for me, my feet almost stumbled,
  my steps nearly slipped.
³ For I envied the arrogant
  (when) I saw the well-being of the wicked. . . .
²⁷ For lo, those far away from you will perish;
  you will silence all those who betray you.
²⁸ But as for me, God's drawing near is good to me;
  I have made the Lord God my refuge. . . .
</blockquote>

The first thing that marks this framing section as noteworthy is the variation in names for the deity. In two of the five verses, four different names occur: El, Elohim, Adonai, and Yahweh. Within the entire psalm only four other direct references to God can be found; El appears twice (vv. 11, 17), Elohim (v. 26) and Elyon (v. 11) once each. The names seem to be chosen carefully, as if to enhance the theological significance of the psalm. The initial statement about divine justice refers to El and Elohim, appropriate names inasmuch as the creedal assertion probably derives from hoary antiquity. The final affirmation moves beyond the general name for God, which it utters first, to special nomenclature that belonged solely to the chosen people (Adonai, Yahweh). When one speaks about a personal refuge, such language of intimacy is entirely appropriate.

A second prominent feature of the framework to the psalm is the carefully designed focus on two distinct entities, the psalmist and the wicked. The introduction announces the slippery ground underneath the psalmist's feet and leads into an allusion to the source of that uneasy footing, the wicked who prosper. The conclusion declares that God will put the quietus on all who remove themselves from the divine presence and betray trust, and subsequently reports that God's nearness suffices to secure slippery feet. That must surely be the implication of the significant metaphor for the Lord: the refuge. The ABB'A' form of vv. 2 and 3 suggests that the circle is closed and that the original affirmation has survived the fiery test.

The Temptation: Prosperity of the Wicked (73:4-12)

⁴ For they have no pangs;
· their bodies are whole *(lāmô tām)* and well nourished.
⁵ They do not experience trouble like ordinary people,
  and are not smitten along with other humans.
⁶ Therefore pride is their necklace;
  violence covers them like a garment.
⁷ Their eyes proceed from abundance;
  wild imaginations pass through their minds.
⁸ They descend into the depth and speak malice;
  from on high they declare oppression.
⁹ They place their mouth in heaven,
  and their tongue walks on earth.

¹⁰ Therefore the people return hither
    and sip abundant waters for themselves.
¹¹ They say, "How can God know?
    Is there knowledge in the Most High?"
¹² Lo, these are the sinners;
    ever at ease, they amass a fortune.

The description of the wicked people who occasion the psalmist's crisis of faith is standard fare, for the most part. We must acknowledge that all such characterizations of the wicked are partial truths. They can hardly be otherwise, for the information they divulge is gathered from a distance. It thus lacks an important ingredient, the actual perceptions of those who suffer from characterization by unsympathetic reporters. It may well be that their lives are not entirely free from care, for the heart alone knows its own suffering (Prov 14:10). Nevertheless, there is enough truth in the account to indicate that these prosperous individuals posed a genuine threat to the community of the faithful.

Precisely what do they say and do that separates them from the psalmist? First, they deny any special relationship with God. That is the import of their twofold question about divine knowledge of terrestrial affairs. Even their use of the epithet Elyon, the Most High, suggests that the deity is far removed from earth and consequently not interested in human doings.[14] Or perhaps God is incapable of discovering what transpires far away. Naturally this claim would negate the fundamental premise of biblical revelation. If it were true, Israel's entire history had been founded on a lie, for at the very heart of her faith lay the conviction that the Lord chose her and set her apart to become a people with whom the deity dwelt in a special way. This could have been possible only if God possessed accurate knowledge about events involving the chosen nation.

The second thing these wicked people do is equally heinous. They

14. Werner E. Lemke ("The Near and the Distant God: A Study of Jer. 23:23-24 in Its Biblical Theological Context," *JBL* 100 [1981]: 541-55) traces the semantic range of *qārōb* and *rāḥôq* in the Hebrew Bible. His analysis of Jeremiah's "free" rendering of the words points to the prophet's desire to break away from a rigid understanding of God that had become popular in certain circles. For further discussion of God's nearness, see A. Caquot, "Psaume LXXIII," *Sem* 21 (1971): 29-55; and Sheldon H. Blank, "The Nearness of God and Psalm Seventy-Three," in *To Do and to Teach: Essays in Honor of Charles Lynn Pratt*, ed. R. M. Pierson (Lexington, Ky.: College of the Bible, 1953), pp. 1-13.

entice multitudes to leave the path of faith in favor of a way that promises richer dividends. To be sure, we cannot tell for certain just what
v. 10 means. Clearly the people try to claim their rightful share in the
prosperity enjoyed by the wicked. They may even heap praises on these
rich folk and drink from the same overflowing fountain. If this is the
meaning of the obscure Hebrew, then the people are bent on pitching
their tent in the midst of faithless ones. No wonder the final punishment awaiting these persons who lead others astray employs a term for
apostasy (zôneh, v. 27).[15] For this grave offense the penalty was death.

The imagery in this section of the psalm is particularly striking. It
is difficult to imagine a better way of saying that pride and violence had
become second nature to these people. These two attributes are like the
clothes they wear and the ornaments with which they adorn themselves. Since malice has an unfathomable quality about it, the association with the depths is understandable. Oppression, however, usually
falls from above, for its perpetrators are persons who possess sufficient
power to crush their opponents. The bizarre picture of a huge creature
with its mouth firmly set in the heavens and its tongue strutting on the
earth seems to echo a description in a Canaanite text.[16] It also resembles a biblical proverb about the destructive power of slander.

The image of eyes peering from behind extraordinarily fat folds of
skin scarcely impresses modern readers, who value slender figures far
more than ancient Israelites did. Behind these healthy eyes was an active mind through which flitted all sorts of evil machinations. Because
the whole body was sound (tām) and well nourished (bārī'), this wishful
thinking was promptly implemented.

It vexes the psalmist no end that such people accumulate a fortune.
Completely undisturbed by want, disease, or misfortune of any kind,
they persist in asking if religion is really worth the bother. In their own
lives there is no room for God, and they seem none the worse for their
abandoning of the faith. The power of pragmatism forges its way into
the central position. Just as Jeremiah's compatriots in Egyptian exile in-

15. The prophet Hosea uses this theme of harlotry with great effectiveness, especially since categories of nature religion were operative during his day.

16. Hans-Joachim Kraus (Psalmen, BKAT 15 [Neukirchen-Vluyn: Neukirchener
Verlag, 1966], 1:506) credits Helmer Ringgren with the comparison. For the Canaanite
text, see Corpus des tablettes en cunéiformes alphabétiques, ed. A. Herder, 23:61-62 ("a lip to
earth and a lip to the heavens").

sisted on applying a pragmatic test to religion and concluded that Yahwism could not survive the competition with the Queen of Heaven, so
here the psalmist's foes elevated the practical above the spiritual. For
them anything that paid huge dividends deserved total allegiance. It
seemed to the psalmist that worship of the Lord no longer yielded a
worthwhile reward. This perception is the lesson acquired from the
wicked, and it needed to be tested in the flames of faith. Here in the divine sanctuary such doubting thoughts could be fully exposed. Until
that ultimate test became a reality, the hostile attitude toward traditional insight would create a nightmare existence for the psalmist.

The Temptation to Abandon a Life of Purity (73:13-16)

13 Entirely in vain have I cleansed my heart
   and washed my hands in innocence.
14 For I suffer torment throughout the day,
   am chastened in the morning.
15 If I had dared to say, "I shall proclaim such things,"
   I would have betrayed the generation of your children.
16 But when I pondered the way to understand this,
   it was burdensome in my sight.

From this brief section we learn that the psalmist takes religious ritual seriously. Yet the external rite of washing the hands was preceded by
an internal purification of the heart. Here we witness a balance between
external observance and inner attitude. The manner of expression links
them together as if that were the natural thing to do. First one purifies
the heart, then one participates in the public ritual. Such is the insight
that also came as prophetic legacy. Men and women who spoke in behalf
of the deity demanded that the hands and heart be cleansed before daring to approach God's altar or lifting up one's voice in prayer.

What then is wrong with the musing to which we are privy through
the psalmist's generosity? Was the twofold religious act wholly in vain?
It would certainly seem so, for the faithfulness to God was rewarded by
unrelenting suffering. We cannot ascertain whether the suffering was
purely mental, the result of anxiety about fading religious convictions.
The pain may well have been physical also. Afflictions thus draw the

psalmist into the circle that produced what we today conveniently label the "suffering servant" theology.

So intense was the discomfort and so fixed was the tradition that the psalmist flirted momentarily with dissimulation. On the one hand, religious conviction had collapsed: God was not good to the pure in heart. This was the conclusion that pressed itself on the suffering author with compelling force. On the other hand, that individual staunchly refused to declare this insight to anyone who might find its allure too much to withstand. What path could the psalmist walk? The one that was reserved for persons who privately believe one thing and proclaim publicly something altogether different? The virtue of this approach was that the family of the Lord remained intact.

However, honesty thrust the psalmist along a more difficult path. That was the journey into the unknown and unfamiliar, where the terrain became one great source of misfortune. The attempt to understand the meaning of this enigma seemed destined to futility. Once more the cry of resignation beckoned: *Entirely in vain* have I pondered a way to understand." But it lost out to a voice that had nothing in common with Qoheleth.

The Turning Point (73:17)

> Until I went into the sanctuary of God,
>   (and) I understood their fate.

Outside the sanctuary events tended to deceive. Only in the presence of God and the community of faith did light begin to dawn: The present moment is not the decisive one in calculating whether the deity is smiling in approval or burning with anger. Divine patience may permit sinners to follow their desires unmolested. Therefore one's perspective must be lengthened to take into account the entire life span. The occasion and manner of one's death may alter the view we take of that person's total existence.[17]

The emphasis falls on the final moment (*'aḥᵃrît*), which I have ren-

---

17. That is the reason Ben Sira was able to advise against pronouncing anyone blessed prior to death.

dered "fate." This translation is entirely appropriate so long as it is divested of any notion of fate with a capital letter. The context is Hebraic, not Greek. For these wicked persons a prosperous life will in the end collapse around them, exposing them to misery such as they have hitherto beheld only in others.

Now at last the burden of trying to understand vanishes. Whereas earlier efforts to grasp the mystery had produced only a cry of resignation and anguish, this new setting opens previously closed windows and allows fresh air to flow freely. The psalmist, as it were, takes a deep breath and shouts the discovery. The key is their fate (*'aḥᵃrîtām*).

"What is there to get excited about?" we ask. Has not this insight been around for generations? Surely the psalmist was not wholly uninformed with regard to the religious reflections of prophets, sages, and priestly instructors. Naturally, one of the first ways of dealing with the problem of theodicy was to recognize compassion in the deity. In short, sinners thrive because God grants them sufficient time to repent of their transgressions. If Psalm 73 has a contribution to make, it cannot be at this point. Where then does that advance in spirituality come?

Of one thing we can be certain. The fresh insight has something to do with a place. Here it is identified as a sacred spot, presumably the temple, but the decisive thing concerns a relationship that blossoms in that holy environment. We can only guess how the psalmist became convinced of divine presence and counsel. Was it by means of a priestly oracle of salvation?[18] Did a prophetic mediator utter a word of the Lord? Or did the assurance come directly to the worshipper? Regardless of the actual manner by which inner renewal came about, a change is apparent. The burden is lifted, and the psalmist proceeds to tell others what is now certain.

The Fate of the Wicked (73:18-20)

> [18] Truly you set them in slippery places;
>   you make them fall to deceptions.
> [19] How quickly they are destroyed;
>   they are utterly swept away by calamity.

18. Joachim Begrich, "Das Priesterliche Heilsorakel," *ZAW* 11-12 (1953): 81-92.

²⁰ Like a dream when the Lord awakes;
   on awakening, you despise their phantoms.

The first thing is that the prosperity of the wicked is unreal. They resemble figments of the imagination conjured up while asleep, and they will vanish just as quickly. Their end is assured; that is the intent of the Hebrew exclamation 'ak (truly). In this instance, as also in v. 1, the particle takes us to the world of confession. This I believe: God will place sinners' feet where not even a toehold can be found. Consequently they will slip into oblivion. Once envied, these unfortunate individuals are now objects of pity. Their insubstantiality is emphasized in the rare word maššú'ôt, which literally means "deceptions." Perhaps it is an allusion to their actual function in misleading the psalmist; perchance it also points forward to an image of figures in a dream that the author intends to develop momentarily.

A subtle change takes place in this verse. The psalmist directs these remarks to God rather than to human beings, who have so far been the target of speech. The first creedal affirmation was about what the deity does; this one addresses God directly. "Surely you will set them on slippery ground" is significantly different from "Surely God is good to the upright, to those whose hearts are pure." This shift is decisive for the insights that slowly emerge toward the end of the psalm.

It is possible that the change to direct address of the deity produced the bold description of the Lord rousing from slumber. Now and again Israel's laments dared to speculate that God was napping, for the world had fallen into the hands of violent people. This unorthodox explanation for the prevalence of injustice may rest behind the psalmist's introduction of the word 'adōnai in connection with awakening from a dream. It seems to the author that the sinners are no more than characters in a divine dream.[19] It follows that they disappear when the Lord rouses from sleep. From the fact that the text reads "You despise their form," we conclude that the psalmist has in mind an unpleasant dream. The sinners who occasioned such consternation are actually no more than fleeting images in a divine nightmare.

19. Buber, "The Heart Determines (Psalm 73)," p. 204.

Resurging Trust in God's Goodness (73:21-26)

21 When my heart was embittered,
    and my inner being was pierced,
22 I was stupid and unknowing;
    I was like Behemoth before you.
23 But I am continually with you;
    you hold me by my right hand.
24 You lead me by your counsel,
    and afterward you receive me [in] honor.
25 Whom have I in heaven [but you],
    and besides you I desire nothing on earth.
26 My flesh and my heart may waste away;
    God is my rock and portion forever.

The poisoning of the mind and nagging doubt transformed the psalmist into a different person. Indeed, the change was so drastic that the word "person" no longer seemed appropriate. Rather, imagery of beasts dominates the description of the author's inner state. The first reference is to their ignorance over against humans; the second recalls their utter defiance of men and women who try to exercise control over them. For the first allusion, one thinks of Agur's ruthless self-criticism preserved in Prov 30:2:

Surely I am more stupid than ordinary mortals,
    and I lack human understanding.[20]

The second reference may be a faint echo of the divine speeches in Job, where Behemoth cavorts in the deep waters, defying humans by its extraordinary power. There is therefore no compelling reason to follow the Septuagint and change *bᵉhēmôt* to *bᵉhēmāh*, the singular form for beast. Anyone who questions God's goodness presumes to know more than is accessible to mere mortals, and whoever dares to challenge God would do well to possess Behemoth's attributes.

20. For analysis of this text, see Paul Franklyn, "The Sayings of Agur in Proverbs 30: Piety or Scepticism?" *ZAW* 95 (1983): 238-52; and James L. Crenshaw, "Clanging Symbols," in *Urgent Advice and Probing Questions* (Macon, Ga.: Mercer University Press, 1995), pp. 371-82.

Having entered the sanctuary, the psalmist has become a new creature. The ignorance has disappeared, and so has the brutish stance before God. Now the picture is a domestic scene of a child and parent
walking hand in hand. Divine presence is envisioned not as sporadic
but as continual. The ancient promise "I shall be with you always" has
become a reality in the psalmist's life. This reality is so tangible that the
only thing that communicates such certainty is the simple yet powerful
thought of an extended hand and the resulting touch. Comforted by
the sensation of warm blood coursing through the veins and making
vital contact with the source of life itself, the psalmist knows that the
path will henceforth be sure. Therefore the psalmist achieves a new
level of confidence: "You lead me by your counsel." Where that leadership takes the psalmist remains a mystery. What is meant by the enigmatic declaration "And afterward you receive me [in] honor"?

As in Job 19:26, we encounter here the adverb *'aḥar* (afterward) —
but after what? After death? At the end of God's leadership? And what
is the sense of the verb *tiqqāḥēnî* (you receive me)? Does it intentionally
invite reflection on the mysterious disappearance of Enoch, who
"walked with God and was not, for God took him" (Gen 5:24)? Finally,
how does the word *kābôd* function here? Does it imply that the psalmist
is assured a good reputation because of continued divine presence, or
does "honor" point beyond death to some kind of existence with God?

Perhaps the next verse supplies a clue for understanding this cryp-
tic reference to being received [in] honor. The psalmist's transformation is total; earthly things have lost their appeal to one whose eyes are
lifted heavenward. "Whom have I in heaven [but you], and besides you I
desire nothing on earth." Such a one has already opted for divine presence now and forever. The overwhelming power that has seized the worshipper stirs the heart beyond the wildest imagination, prompting in-
conceivable thought. Mind and body will eventually decay, but is that
the end? If so, that moment will mark the close of a relationship in
which God has been a rock and a portion from the occasion of the
psalmist's visit to the divine sanctuary. But if death does not signal the
end. . . .

The choice of "rock" and "portion" to describe God seems to point
beyond death. The durability of the rock, together with the temporal
expression *lᵉ'ôlām* (unto the ages), would seem to suggest more than the
remaining years allotted to the psalmist. The same is true of the word

ḥelqî (my portion), which in the narrative tradition applied to a gift that passed from generation to generation. The land of Canaan was Israel's portion, and that gift did not become null and void with the death of the first generation of God's people. To be sure, the word *ḥelqî* is used frequently in Qoheleth with an entirely different sense,[21] but Ps 73:26 lacks the slightest hint of such negative thoughts. Whereas for Qoheleth the portion may be something to complain about, here it is nothing less than divine presence. The psalmist has stood near the flame and has at last been caught up in it.[22]

FURTHER READING

Nielsen, Eduard. "Psalm 73: Scandinavian Contributions." In *Understanding Poets and Prophets: Essays in Honour of George Wishart Anderson*, ed. A. G. Auld, pp. 273-83. JSOTSS 152. Sheffield: JSOT, 1993.

21. James Williams, "What Does It Profit a Man?: The Wisdom of Koheleth," *Judaism* 20 (1971): 179-93, reprinted in *Studies in Ancient Israelite Wisdom*, ed. James L. Crenshaw (New York: KTAV, 1976), pp. 375-89, esp. pp. 384-86.

22. The answer to the psalmist's heart-rending problem comes from religious faith and personal experience at worship, not from discussion with sages in the vicinity of the temple. That is the chief reason for questioning James F. Ross's explanation for the psalmist's insight as the result of attending to scholarly debate ("Psalm 73," pp. 167-69).

CHAPTER EIGHT

The Resounding Negation: Psalm 115

1 Not to us, Yahweh, not to us, but to your name give glory,
   because of your loving-kindness and integrity.
2 Why should the nations say,
   "Where is their God?"
3 Surely our God is in heaven;
   whatever he wants, he does.
4 Their gods are silver and gold,
   the work of human hands.
5 They have mouths but cannot speak,
   eyes but cannot see.
6 They have ears but cannot hear,
   noses but cannot smell.
7 They have hands but cannot feel,
   feet but cannot walk.
 No sound rises from their throats.
8 Their makers are like them,
   all those who trust in them.
9 Israel, trust in Yahweh;
   he is their help and shield.
10 House of Aaron, trust in Yahweh;
   he is their help and shield.
11 Those who fear Yahweh, trust in Yahweh;
   he is their help and shield.
12 May Yahweh remember us and bless. . . .

> May he bless the house of Israel;
>> may he bless the house of Aaron.
> 13 May he bless those who fear Yahweh,
>> both small and great.
> 14 May Yahweh add to you,
>> to you and your children.
> 15 Blessed are you to Yahweh,
>> maker of heaven and earth.
> 16 The highest heaven belongs to Yahweh,
>> but he has entrusted the earth to mortals.
> 17 The dead do not praise Yah,
>> nor any who go down to Silence.
> 18 But we ourselves do bless Yah from now on. Hallelujah.

Israel's struggle against the worship of false gods can be traced to its beginning when, according to a tradition preserved in the book of Exodus, the people persuaded Aaron to fashion a golden bull before which they could bow down in homage. With the memory of this shameful incident still fresh, Joshua calls on those entering the land of promise to join him and his house in rejecting all other gods and pledging absolute allegiance to Yahweh. Like Martin Luther, who spoke these courageous words, "Here I stand; I can do no other: God help me," Moses' successor witnesses through personal example rather than by rhetoric alone.

The people's wish to have a god who did not disappear for days on end is perfectly understandable. So is the endeavor to manipulate the deity for personal gain, but a hiding god renders such efforts futile. Yahweh's refusal to allow anyone to gain control over the sacred name meant that access to the deity remained in divine hands: that is, the Lord freely chose when to become present to Israel and its leaders. Confronted by such a deity, the people developed a cultic apparatus and chose priestly leaders to break through the barrier resulting from Yahweh's freedom and to appropriate divine blessing. From their perspective, this priestly hierarchy owed its origin to divine initiative.

The evolution of idolatry may be adequately explained by Ludwig Feuerbach's theory of projection. People create gods in their own image and project them on the heavens, he argued, bowing down to the work of their own imagination and in the end paying homage to themselves.

The peoples of the ancient Near East fashioned statues in human form and worshipped them as the deity's visible representation. In contrast to this type of idolatry, Israel's venture in making its own god took the form of a golden bull. The care with which the gods were treated among Israel's neighbors attests to the high regard in which they were held, even if everyone knew them to be the works of human hands. In the minds of these people their statues pointed beyond themselves to a reality far greater, which we today call God.

Israel's polemic against the practice of worshipping God by means of visual objects ignores this reality, even though the ark comes perilously close to the practices abhorred in this literature. Presumably, it functioned as the pedestal for an invisible Yahweh, who could not be represented visually by anything in heaven or on earth. This aniconism — rejection of religious icons — is unparalleled in the ancient world. We do not know how widespread this stand against religious icons was, although it did not extend to the masses in Israel, who seem to have followed the practice of worshipping many gods in visible form.

Nothing seems more natural than the adoration of the hidden by means of the visible. That is why the explanations for idolatry make sense in this polemical literature. A grieving father carves a likeness of his dead son, a patriotic citizen makes an image that reminds him of a distant king, a gifted artist creates a work that evokes gratitude for beauty itself. In each of these plausible explanations that appear in Wisdom of Solomon we catch a fleeting glimpse of powerful emotions — grief, patriotism, passion — that often accompany worship.

The role of grief in worship can be traced to early myths about the death of seasonal gods. Its power persists in the Christian drama of death and resurrection. The interweaving of patriotism and religion has a long history too, for ancient peoples believed that their gods rose and fell with the fortunes of the empire. Artistic offerings to the gods have existed from earliest times, for persons with extraordinary talent have always sought to communicate to others their own vision of a deeper reality than the one seen by ordinary eyes.

Precisely because the reasons for using images in worship commended themselves to religious people, Israel's champions of the aniconic ideal were unrelenting in their absolute disapproval of the practice. A balanced appraisal of their polemic would condemn these authors for falsifying the nature of the worship under attack, but the authors would probably have justified their actions by pointing to the high stakes involved. In their view the survival of Yahwistic worship lay in the balances, and it was worth saving at any cost.

One did not need to be a genius to recognize the vulnerability of idols to ridicule. Gods fashioned in human form naturally lent themselves to mockery on the basis of weaknesses inherent to mortals. Despite the coating of precious metals, exquisite design and color, ornate clothing, and courtly paraphernalia provided for them, the gods depended on humans for everything. At times the ridicule could be merciless, at other times, downright humorous. Thieves can steal defenseless gods, impure women can handle them, birds can defecate on them. For protection on a journey, one prays to a god that cannot take a single step. The same piece of wood produces a god, a tool, and warmth from a fire. Deceptive priests mislead the public into thinking the gods consume the offerings brought to them, and an exposed idol explodes in their faces like the myth perpetrated by their custodians. This sampling of Israel's relentless attack on idols indicates the ease with which they could be ridiculed. The remarkable tenacity of idol worshippers in the face of such mockery ought to alert us to the human longing for representation of the divine.

The ancient tradition that God created mortals in the divine image might encourage the belief that we behold the deity in ourselves, except for the strong emphasis on transcendence in the priestly narrative. In any event, the notion that we resemble the Creator in some sense, whether in our supremacy over the earth, or in our cognitive self-transcendence, or in our ability to communicate verbally, encourages those who would fashion objects in human form for religious purposes. This impulse to worship the unseen by means of the visible enables us to recognize deep within the human psyche an imperative of wonder. No amount of ridicule can obscure this important intuition.

The author of Psalm 115 participates in the struggle for authentic worship and perpetuates the tradition of ridiculing images in human shape. The battle is waged on a much broader front, however, for the psalm issues a resounding negation of the human tendency to bask in its own greatness. Like Psalm 8, which gives voice to the notion that mortals rank slightly lower than heavenly beings, although without forgetting the exalted place of God, this psalm ultimately praises Yahweh. A cursory glance at human achievements seems to support a high estimate of mortals, as the words attributed to the deity in the story about the tower of Babel imply ("Look, they are one people and have a single language . . . and nothing is beyond their power," Gen 11:6). Faced with such grandiosity, the psalmist begins and ends with a reminder that true adoration comes to rest in the Lord, not in human beings.

> Not to us, Yahweh, not to us, but to your name give glory,
>> Because of your loving-kindness and integrity.   (v. 1)

> But we . . . let us bless Yahweh from now on.
>> Hallelujah.
>>   (v. 18)

Both the inverted syntax and the redundancy in the opening verse call into question the praising of mortals, while the central position of Yahweh between the two negations points to the proper object of adoration. The poet holds in abeyance the object of concern, letting the word "glory" appear last in the colon. The heavens may be full of Yahweh's glory, but this psalmist thinks the earth should resound with a similar sound, and that the deity should not shrink from self-praise.

That is exactly what occurs in the memorable story recorded in Exod 34:1-8, which the psalmist apparently has in mind when citing two of the divine attributes, loving-kindness and truth, as the basis for ascribing glory to Yahweh. The thirteen uses of the name Yahweh in the psalm correspond to the number of attributes that Yahweh calls to Moses' attention. The traditional means of protecting divine mystery by substituting concepts like face and name persists in this psalm. Each of these qualities functions as a kind of alter ego of Yahweh for the Priestly author and the Deuteronomist, respectively. In Deut 12:5 Yahweh promises to put the divine name in the sanctuary, probably Shechem but later thought to mean Jerusalem. That name would, in the belief of the author, assure Yahweh's presence at all times. In the same way the face of Yahweh was thought to have accompanied Israel in the wilderness.

The psalmist's concern for Yahweh's reputation is not entirely altruistic, as the second verse makes abundantly clear.

> Why should the nations say, "Where is their God?"

Here in a few words is the fundamental problem of saving face when historical circumstances do not appear to support theological belief. Victory in battle enables a people to look on its deity as supreme, whereas defeat implies weakness on the part of the patron deity. Similarly, disaster of every kind opened the door for detractors to mock the victims by making fun of their protective powers. In Israel's case the protector was Yahweh, and to all appearances this deity was in the course of history shown to be impotent before the great gods of Assyria, Babylon, and Persia. In the case of the psalmist this painful question is still hypothetical; the sentence could be translated "Lest the nations exclaim, 'Where is their God?'" The question, posed by one foreigner to another, lacks the acrimony of the taunting word directed to the victims themselves. The psalmist frets about the effect of Yahweh's diminishing reputation on foreigners; they are strengthened in their conviction that Yahweh lacks the power to defend Israelites.

In Psalms 42–43 this question carries a bitter sting because it falls on the psalmist's ears. The twice-repeated "While they say to me continually, 'Where is your God?'" is balanced by a threefold refrain acknowledging the deleterious effect of such mockery on the poet's psyche. At the same time the psalmist refuses to surrender to despair ("Why are you so low, my soul, and why so disturbed? Hope in God, for I shall praise him once more, my savior and my God"). The suppliant's deep longing for God matches the profound sense of loss resulting from the deity's absence. Here, too, Yahweh's integrity has come into question, prompting the psalmist to ask for help in the form of the divine light and truth (43:3).

The author of Psalm 115 exercises more restraint than this because the question "Where is their God?" comes from within. The answer seems obvious:

> Surely our God is in heaven;
> whatever he wants, he does.   (v. 3)

At least it was transparent to the poet who composed Psalm 135, for whom the greatness of Yahweh manifested itself in sovereignty over the gods and in implementing the divine will in heaven, on earth, in the seas, and in the depths. As the psalmist states succinctly, "Yahweh does whatever he pleases" (v. 6). This response to the anomalies of history and tests of conviction runs into difficulty when one examines it closely. If true, does the assertion that Yahweh does everything he desires really mean that the Lord does not take delight in bestowing well-being on good people? Yahweh's loving-kindness ought to equal, if not surpass, his power. Divine might means nothing unless harnessed for just, or better still, compassionate, ends.

Acting on the principle that a good offense is the best defense, the psalmist goes on the attack,

> Their gods are silver and gold, the work of human hands.
> They have mouths but cannot speak, eyes but cannot see.
> They have ears but cannot hear, noses but cannot smell.
> They have hands but cannot feel, feet but cannot walk.
> No sound rises from their throats.   (vv. 4-7)

The conclusion, that "their makers are like them, all those who trust in them" (v. 8), emphasizes the paralyzing effect of idolatry on those who practice it. They take on the essential quality of the objects of their affection, in this instance lifelessness. Resembling futility curses, these descriptive phrases drone away, the monotony having the effect of inducing sleep akin to the eternal stupor characterizing the gods themselves. Not only do these works of human hands lack the fundamental capacity bestowed on sentient beings to speak, observe, hear, smell, touch, and walk; they do not even possess the ability to make elemental sounds that communicate emotional distress or dire need. Their impressive exterior of silver and gold cannot compensate for the deficiencies of the senses. What these humaniform objects lack is the divine "breath of life" generously bestowed on the first mortal (Gen 2:7) and subsequently on everyone as a condition of existence for the brief period allotted each. At the final moment, so it was believed, Yahweh reclaimed the precious life breath.

For what audience was this realistic description of idols intended? Not the actual owners of these artifacts, whether foreigners or Israelites, for both the medium and the message suggest that the attack on idolatry functions to strengthen the Yahwistic community rather than to undercut those who placed their hope on other gods. The location of the mockery within a psalm gives it a thoroughly devotional flavor, and the argument aims at convincing those loyal to Yahweh that idols had no substance beyond external appearance. The brief unit assured the people that devotion to idols would bring them nothing worthwhile.

Amazingly, biblical literature in this vein overlooks an obvious objection for those who insist that their God cannot be seen: the deity cannot be seen because it does not exist. In a polytheistic environment like that of the ancient Near East an absolute denial of theism never seems to occur to anyone, unless Agur in Proverbs 30 actually goes that far. The closest that others come to the absolute position of atheism is typically clothed in a question pertaining either to power or to presence ("Can God see . . . Where is their God?"). Occasionally, a polemicist against radical thinking will articulate the question of questions, always attributed to a fool. For this hapless individual the interrogative form has given way to the declarative, as if an answer in the negative has been found ("There is no God!"). The opposite predilection occurs when people erect an inscription to the unknown God, believing that the inability to see deity does not disprove the unseen reality.

A single word stands out in the final apposition comprising the last colon in verse 8. That word, "trust," becomes the theme of the following unit.

> Israel, trust in Yahweh; he is their help and shield.
> House of Aaron, trust in Yahweh; he is their help and shield.
> Fearers of Yahweh, trust in Yahweh; he is their help and shield.
>
> (vv. 9-11)

A shift in speakers seems to take place here. Until this point the entire congregation appears to be pouring out its collective soul to Yahweh. Now a priestly voice may be heard, urging everyone present at the holy place to trust in Yahweh and grounding that admonition in the Lord's ability to protect his own people.

The brief unit has a distinctly liturgical character, particularly the direct address to three different groups, the imperative forms, and the refrain that concludes each one. The present vocalization of the Hebrew text presents problems, however, for those who understand the imperatives as priestly exhortation. The third person plural suffixes on "help" and "shield" make more sense if we read the verbs as finite: "Israel has trusted in Yahweh; he is their help and shield" and so on. Otherwise we expect second person pronominal suffixes: "He is your help and shield." The initial position of the nouns in the first colon of each verse favors the interpretation above: that they constitute vocatives.

Who were these three groups? The first one, Israel, includes the entire congregation, presumably the Judean community in the exilic or postexilic period. If this assumption is correct, the people have probably come to a local synagogue to worship Yahweh. The second group, singled out from the larger entity, consists of the priestly leaders, here designated the house of Aaron. The final group, those who fear Yahweh, probably is made up of foreigners who have gravitated to the local community of Jews who worship Yahweh. The attraction may have been the result of intermarriage; alternatively, intellectual and spiritual affinities with Yahwism may have drawn them to the place of worship, like the later god-fearers. The Septuagint uses that expression to translate "fearers of Yahweh" in verse 11. On this reading, the third group consisted of proselytes. One could, however, understand the reference as inclusive, like the earlier "Israel." The movement would then be from the entire congregation to a select group within it and then finally to the congregation once more. In terms of poetic scansion, the three vocatives would yield an ABA form.

The language of the second colon belongs to warfare. Yahweh stands ready to assist the worshipper in battle and to shield one and all from dangerous missiles. The litany, only three words in Hebrew, does not vary. Three times the pronoun "he" concludes the affirmation: their help and shield — he. Behind this pronoun one should probably hear Yahweh's self-identification in Deutero-Isaiah ("I am he"), which may refer to a numinous exclamation that the hidden deity now manifest in cultic theophany is truly "That One."

The first three words in the Hebrew of verse 12 do not inaugurate a new psalm, as many manuscripts indicate, but mark a shift in perspective. The vocatives and imperatives give way to jussives, as the speaker indirectly implores Yahweh to bestow blessing on the three aforementioned groups within the congregation.

May Yahweh remember us and bless . . .   (v. 12a)

The invocation of these two verbs links the present assembly with past generations to whom a promise of blessing was first made and offers a hint that things have not gone well. Yahweh had promised to bless

Abraham and his descendants, making them as numerous as the sands on the seashore and stars in the sky, but now the number of Abraham's descendants had dwindled. Furthermore, the land that they understood to be their legacy from Yahweh had fallen into alien hands, making recovery of it a slow and difficult process. To all appearances, Yahweh had forgotten those earlier promises.

Each of the verbs falls into the category of Israel's theological vocabulary. The act of remembering calls to mind a relationship in the past, and the fact that someone intentionally evokes former experience suggests that the memory will be pleasant. In times past a mutual bond, a covenant, linked the people with Yahweh. This relationship implied reciprocity of action: loyalty on Israel's part and protection on Yahweh's part. Hence the speaker's gentle reminder, "May Yahweh remember," presupposes the Lord's readiness to recall the promises of long ago. Similarly, the blessing emerges from the same context of mutual love. From the human side, blessing demands pure praise of the Lord, who responds by bestowing the good things that make life possible and pleasant.

The pronominal suffix changes at this point from third to first person plural; *their* is replaced by *us,* and the speaker increases the intimacy of the language. The previous distance between liturgist and congregation vanishes and they become one. It returns in verses 14-15, only to give way in verse 18 to a sense of oneness. The sudden use of personal pronouns in verses 15 and 18 instead of suffixes emphasizes this extraordinary shift in perspective.

The verb "bless" has no suffix, although the suffix on the previous verb may have a double function. The result of the missing object amounts to an ellipsis; the priestly benediction then supplies what has as yet remained unspoken:

> May he bless the house of Israel; may he bless the house of Aaron;
> May he bless the fearers of Yahweh, both small and great.
>
> (vv. 12b and 13)

The language recalls the fuller priestly benediction in Num 6:24-26:

> May Yahweh bless you and watch over you;
> May Yahweh smile upon you and be gracious to you;
> May Yahweh show you favor and give you peace.

The rich theological vocabulary in so compact a setting, scarcely matched elsewhere, has greatly enriched the liturgy of Judaism and Christianity. The three groups in verses 12-13 correspond to those called upon in verses 9-11 to place their hope in Yahweh. Their faithfulness, together with Yahweh's remembrance, paves the way for divine blessing. The merism, both small and great, describes the hoped-for benefits as inclusive. Neither infants nor the aged will miss out on the boon. Alternatively, no social class will be excluded, whether those of low estate or persons of high status. This impulse toward total inclusivity reaches its pinnacle in the well-known prophetic oracle in Joel 2:28-29 [MT 3:1-2].

> Afterwards I will endow all of you with my vital force,
> so that your boys and girls will speak oracles on my behalf;
> your old people will discern my will through dreams,
> and your young adults will become visionaries.
> On your slaves, too, both male and female,
> I will bestow my vital force at that time.

Like Joel, the psalmist does not wish to see anyone in the assembled congregation miss out on the blessings of Yahweh.

As if to recall the ancient promise to Abraham, the psalmist adds a specific benediction in verse 14.

> May Yahweh add to you, to you and your children.

The decimation of the postexilic community as a result of warfare, plague, starvation, and disease had become a grim reality. In the face of diminishing numbers, the people struggled to survive. The request that Yahweh increase their number arises from prior conviction that conception and birth cannot take place without divine approval. It was believed that Yahweh closed the womb and opened it, that the mystery of birth entailed Yahweh's own handiwork. Curiously, the psalmist adopts a stance somewhat removed from the ones on whom the blessing falls. Here the pronominal suffix "you" returns, perhaps as a requirement of the liturgical style.

The following hymnic verse balances Israel's worth with Yahweh's majesty, although the people are seen from the perspective of the one to whom they belong:

Blessed are you to Yahweh, maker of heaven and earth.   (v. 15)

The thematic verb *bless* now occurs in the form of a predicate adjective describing the congregation, which has taken on the quality of divine blessing. The syntax reinforces the idea of ownership; Israel belongs to Yahweh precisely because it can claim a favored status. Moreover, the anticipated blessing has become reality, perhaps the result of a priestly oracle of salvation. Yahweh has heard the priest's request and has responded favorably. A needy people has now undergone transformation. A single word conveys that change: *blessed.* The *you* characterized by this adjective applies to the house of Israel, the house of Aaron, and those who fear Yahweh. Israelites, priestly leaders, and proselytes stand in a favored relationship before Yahweh.

The participial construction, "maker of heaven and earth," widens the scope of Yahweh's possessions to include the entire universe, not just the covenanted people. The language has the ring of a confession, so it is no surprise that the brief expression eventually found its way into the Apostles' Creed of the Early Church. Elsewhere in the Psalter the confession has gravitated to the Songs of Ascent (120–134), where it occurs three times (121:2; 124:8; 134:3). The first two of these texts associate the expression, "maker of heaven and earth," with Yahweh's readiness to help the psalmist and assembled people. That same notion occurs in Ps 115:9-11, also a liturgical confession ("He is their help and shield"). Who could question the ability of the maker of heaven and earth to provide help in all circumstances? The third occurrence of the phrase in the Songs of Ascent takes the form of a priestly blessing: "May Yahweh bless you from Zion, maker of heaven and earth" (134:3). The physical location of Yahweh at Jerusalem implies that the Creator has chosen the holy city as the place from which divine blessing flows.

The next verse in Psalm 115 imitates the syntax of the preceding one in the first colon but diverges from the hymnic style of the second colon.

The highest heaven belongs to Yahweh,
  but he has entrusted the earth to mortals.

This extraordinary observation reflects the hierarchical organization of things in the priestly account of creation (Gen 1:1–2:4a). Here the mastery of the earth by mortals is conveyed not only in a command from God but also in the notion that women and men bear the divine image. The Creator's domain is properly heaven, while mortals are expected to exercise sovereignty over the creatures on earth. The psalmist makes a bold claim that Yahweh's ownership, and therefore sovereignty, reaches down to include the persons deserving of blessing and up to envelop the heavens and their inhabitants, whom mortals call gods.

By no stretch of the imagination does this description of territoriality suggest that Yahweh's authority applies solely to the heavenly realm (cf. Deut 10:14). The psalmist's use of the verb *nātan* (to give) indicates that the control of both regions, heaven and earth, rests ultimately in Yahweh's hands. The earth has simply been handed over to mortals as a kind of trust. The universal expression, children of Adam (mortals), stands out in this setting, which has thus far been restricted to those individuals who worship Yahweh. When the idea of creation enters the discussion, such artificial restrictions fly out the window. The maker of heaven and earth lays claim to every living creature.

The psalmist reverts to convoluted syntax in the final two verses, which contrast two realms of a different kind, the dead and the living.

> The dead do not praise Yah, nor any who go down to Silence.
> But we ourselves do bless Yah from now on. Hallelujah.
>
> (vv. 17-18)

The third region in ancient Near Eastern cosmology comes into play in these verses; Sheol, here called Silence, consists of the subterranean waters and land of the dead. In the opinion of this psalmist, and that of many others (6:6; 30:10; 88:11), those who have departed to Sheol can no longer raise voices in song to Yahweh. In these verses the Lord is identified by the short form Yah. This reluctance to associate Yahweh with the land of the dead may have arisen as resistance to the popular cult of gods connected with the underworld.

The initial negative, separated from its verb by the subject of the sentence, recalls the opening verse ("Not to us, Yahweh, not to us"). A literal rendering — "Not the dead, they bless Yah, and not all who descend to Silence" — exposes the author's ineptness or points to a conscious attempt to form a grammatical inclusio (the practice of returning to the beginning, a well-known feature of biblical poetry). The exclusive use of Yah may suggest an editorial hand.

The psalmist closes on a high note: in contrast to the mute dead, we have the power and desire to praise Yah, and we shall do so from this time forward. The verb *bārak* (to bless) appears once more as if to acknowledge that divine blessings upon a blessed people produce fruit in kind. The emphatic use of the personal pronoun amounts to the total submersion of the liturgist into the congregation. The earlier distinctions, conveyed by alternating pronominal suffixes for second and third person, disappear, and the entire community enters into a solemn promise: "But we ourselves do bless Yah from now on. Hallelujah." In this instance an emphatic negation has given birth to ceaseless praise, not for mortals in their glory but for the maker of heaven and earth, the people's help and shield.

CHAPTER NINE

Life's Deepest Apprehension: Psalm 71

1 In you, Yahweh, I take refuge;
  never let me be ashamed.
2 By your righteous deeds deliver me and rescue me;
  bend your ear to me and save me.
3 Be for me a rocky refuge — you have ordered [me] to
    come regularly — to
  save me, for you are a rocky crag and fortress.
4 My God, rescue me from the power of the wicked,
  from the grasp of the perverse and cruel.
5 For you are my hope, Lord;
  Yahweh, my trust from youth.
6 On you I have leaned from the womb,
  from my mother's belly you extracted me;
  in you is my praise continually.
7 I have become a virtual portent for many,
  but you are my strong refuge.
8 My mouth is full of your praise,
  all day long your wonders.
9 Do not toss me aside in old age;
  when my strength diminishes, do not abandon me.
10 For my enemies say about me,
  "Let us observe him and take common counsel:
11 God has abandoned him;
  pursue and seize him, for he has none to deliver."

12 God, be not distant from me;
    my God, rush to my aid.
13 Let those who oppose me be ashamed and consumed;
      let them be a reproach and disgrace —
    those who seek to hurt me,
14 But I keep on hoping
    and increase your praise.
15 My mouth will recite your righteous works,
    your saving deeds all day long,
    although I do not comprehend their number.
16 I will come in strength, Lord God;
    I will sing of nothing but your righteous deeds.
17 God, you taught me from my youth;
    and until now I proclaim your wonderful works.
18 Even until [I am] old and gray, God,
    do not forsake me,
  until I tell your might to a generation;
    your power to all who come.
19 Your righteous deeds unto the heavens, God,
    in that you have done great things,
    God, who is like you?
20 That you have shown me numerous adversities and evils,
    you will renew me once more;
    and from the depths of the earth you will lift me again.
21 You will increase my honor, embrace me, and comfort me.
22 Also with a harp I will praise you for your faithfulness, my God;
    I will sing about you with a lyre, Holy One of Israel.
23 My lips will sing, indeed I will sing about you,
    I myself, whom you redeemed.
24 My tongue will also meditate throughout the day
      on your righteous deeds,
  for those who seek to hurt me have been shamed and disgraced.

An aging population in the United States has focused attention on the attendant problems, particularly providing adequate health care and maintaining a solvent program in Social Security. The increased cost for medical treatment of older people is staggering, and the decreasing number of employed persons paying funds into the retirement system of the Federal Government has begun to worry people who value fiscal responsibility. Uncertainties over how to address these two issues have raised the level of anxiety that, like poverty, seems omnipresent as a result of violent crime, unemployment, drugs, and other unspecified ills in society. Faced with so many problems, someone would have to be out of touch with reality not to be apprehensive over the future.

The deepest apprehension, however, anxiety that is exacerbated by the accumulation of years, befalls those who sense a decline in strength, a definite signal that the process of death has achieved dominance over that of life. With this realization comes the dawn of something they have always known but see now with fresh eyes: that they will die. They do not know when that moment will arrive, but they understand that its presence will hound them for the rest of their days and nights. In this weakened state, they imagine being alone and vulnerable, for if dying is something no one can do for them, so is growing old. The thought of being tossed aside like useless junk becomes real to the aged who have the misfortune of living in a culture that does not value people in their advanced years. The idea of being abandoned by one's deity at this vulnerable time seems more than anyone can bear. This deepest of all apprehensions gives Psalm 71 immediate recognition among older readers who resonate with the prayer, "Do not toss me aside in old age; when my strength diminishes, do not abandon me" (v. 9).

The idea that Yahweh needs to be reminded not to abandon a loyal subject strikes the reader as strange, in some ways like the petition in the Lord's Prayer that God not lead us into temptation. The thought weighed so heavily on the mind of the psalmist that it elicited a second petition, this time with the familiar combination "old and gray" ("Even until [I am] old and gray, God, do not forsake me" (v. 18a). Experience had taught the psalmist that God's ways are not always fathomable, and this element of unknowability sometimes gave the appearance of indifference or malevolence on God's part. It is precisely when an individual has entered the period of greatest vulnerability that the thought of being left alone to face the unknown can be unnerving, especially when one has had a long history of intimacy with the divine, as here (vv. 5 and 17, from my youth; v. 6, from the womb).

Even if it could be demonstrated that these allusions to waning years constitute metaphors, the apprehension over being abandoned to one's enemies, whatever their nature, gives the psalm universal appeal. The vulnerability of the loner even achieved proverbial status in the ancient Near East, where a saying about a threefold cord emphasized the protection that comes with numbers. The author of Ecclesiastes quotes this proverb and reinforces its teaching with two of his own implying safety and warmth. In his view, a traveling companion can lift a fallen comrade to safety and generate warmth against the chill of the night by lying close (Eccles 4:9-12). Given the importance of human companionship, how much more essential is the divine. Abandonment by the deity at any stage of life therefore bodes ill.

Thus while modern readers resonate with this psalm in its deepest apprehension, they can find little point of contact with the notion of honor and shame underlying the text. Scholars have only recently begun to appreciate the powerful role played by honor and its opposite among ancient residents of the Levant. In Psalm 71 the effort by persons seeking to bring dishonor and reproach on the author prompts the initial prayer for help (vv. 2-3) and an eventual assertion that these same enemies will suffer loss of honor and endure reproach from those whose esteem they solicit (v. 24b).

The urbanization of modern society in the West has made strangers of almost everyone, and honor has become a quaint value of a bygone era. One's profession has become the primary means of achieving stature in the community, and wealth goes a long way toward purchasing societal approval. In the tiny villages of ancient Israel, a person's standing in the eyes of neighbors contributed to or took away from self-esteem. To be put to shame was a horrible thing, and such dishonor came from different areas of life. Children frequently brought honor or shame on their parents, especially through sexual transgression. Faced with rape, Tamar reminded her brother that such a thing is not done in Israel (2 Sam 13:12), and having been so dishonored, she spent the remainder of her life as a living portent. Honor demanded that her family avenge the deed; similarly, Dinah's brothers carried out a sweeping execution of the Shechemites for the shame they brought to their sister and the whole family (Gen 34:25-31). In such a world saving face means everything.

Because sickness was often viewed as punishment for sin, anyone who fell grievously ill also suffered loss of honor. The biblical Job appears to have resented the reproach heaped on him by friends and ruffians more than his physical pain. His precipitate decline in the eyes of neighbors forms the subject of a remarkable account by this victim who still remembers the former days of honor (Job 29-30). Biblical prophets like Joel used the culture of honor and shame to good advantage when faced with a devastating crisis brought on by invading locusts. In the early second century Ben Sira perceived a need to distinguish exactly what things ought to evoke shame, which can be a positive virtue (Sir 41:17–42:8). Psalm 71 does not move in this new direction, but it certainly assumes the binding character of honor and shame. The poet wants to avoid shame at any cost, while also wishing reproach on enemies.

Like most laments, this one freely mentions adversaries (vv. 4, 10-11, 13 and 24b):

> My God, rescue me from the power of the wicked,
>   from the grasp of the perverse and cruel. . . .
> For my enemies say about me,
>   "Let us observe him and take common counsel:
> God has abandoned him;
>   pursue and seize him, for he has none to deliver." . . .
> Let those who oppose me be ashamed and consumed;
>   let them be a reproach and disgrace —
>   those who seek to hurt me. . . .
> For those who seek to hurt me have been shamed and disgraced.

The participial constructions emphasize the ongoing process of a band of antagonists determined to take advantage of one who, in their opinion, has been completely forsaken. Their imagined speech resembles that of brigands in Prov 1:11-14, with the promise of a common purse. Against an isolated victim the consolidation of effort holds great promise. The psalmist's use of the ordinary word for providential care in verse 10 to describe the enemies as observers carries enormous irony when followed immediately by their conclusion that God has abandoned him. Those watching now are bent on his destruction, as the graphic language suggests: run after him and seize him.

The speaker in the psalm is not a stranger to adversity, even apart from these enemies. According to verse 20, the psalmist attributes much calamity to God:

That you have shown me numerous adversities and evils, . . .

This way of describing unpleasant experiences as direct acts of the deity stems from belief in God as the ultimate cause of all things, whether good or bad. The adversities may have been brought on by the above-mentioned enemies, but the psalmist understands God as the one who caused the events to transpire. That being so, God can also reverse the nature of experiences, bringing honor instead of shame. The decisive issue may be a matter of interpretation, as the psalmist recognizes: "I have become a virtual portent for many" (v. 7a). Some viewers interpret the sign positively, others negatively.

Biblical signs and portents point beyond themselves to the hidden work of God, often but not always in the midst of adversity. Sometimes an afflicted individual like Job understands his suffering and disgrace as a portent that misleads others into thinking he has been abandoned by God. Similarly, onlookers construe the cruel treatment of the suffering servant in Deutero-Isaiah as a portent indicating the destiny of transgressors (Isa 53:4). Portents do not have to be human. Frequently, they are identified with extraordinary events in the sky, like eclipses that appear to suspend daylight briefly or to turn night into total blackness. At other times, a portent signifies munificence, a gracious deity at work behind the scenes. Biblical authors interpreted a host of things as signs of Yahweh's favor. These range from private experiences associated with pregnancy to entirely public events like the plagues in Egypt that, according to traditional narrative, spared the enslaved Hebrews but struck the Egyptians.

Signs in themselves are mute. They require an interpreter who reads them in the light of an interpretive tradition. In the case of the psalmist, enemies understand the portent as favorable to them. Apparent abandonment by the deity has left the wretch completely vulnerable. Presumably, they assume that others concur in this assessment of the situation, for they think no one will come to the victim's defense. The rationale for this assumption is obvious. They believe others will hold back from coming to the rescue because aiding him would constitute interference with divine punishment for wrongdoing. The psalmist's discomfiture, as they view it, arises from sin. The context belies their reading of the situation, for the psalmist's repeated affirmation of complete trust in Yahweh that eventuates in the statement equating him with a portent favors a positive interpretation. The faithful worshipper who has relied on Yahweh throughout life stands as a sign of true devotion, a portent that offers encouragement to others who look on God as their refuge.

The poet claims to have received special instruction from the divine teacher. He writes: "God, you taught me from my youth; and until now I proclaim your wonderful works" (v. 17). The content of instruction in early years seems to matter less than the subject filling the mouth of the human instructor. The psalmist promises to proclaim the marvelous deeds of God. The rich vocabulary indicating these accomplishments points to their extraordinary range and nature (wonders, might, power, righteous deeds, and grand things, vv. 17-19). Transmitting this message to succeeding generations becomes a priority for the psalmist, who can point to a long relationship in the service of God.

The awesome works of God that require several Hebrew words to convey their splendor point to a unique deity. The psalmist endeavors to make this point by referring to an inability to recount God's deeds and by asking simply, "God, who is like you?" (vv. 15b and 19b). Yahweh's incomparability occupied the minds of several biblical authors, none so tenaciously as Deutero-Isaiah's. This herald of good tidings sought to demonstrate Yahweh's uniqueness by appealing to the deity's foreknowledge and ability to shape events as planned long ago. The Creator of heaven and earth defeated the mythic beasts of primordial times and delivered the Israelites from their jaws, empowering his people to march forth into the land of promise. This historicization of mythic lore brought into prominence every specific incident out of the ordinary, which gradually took on the character of a soteriological deed, a saving act.

Such flattering rhetoric belongs to religion in general, for worshippers quite naturally believe that their deity alone deserves full allegiance. The god being invoked possesses wisdom, power, integrity, and compassion — precisely those qualities that human beings value. Like religious people throughout the ancient Near East, the psalmist gladly volunteered to help disseminate the word about the deity's heroic exploits. Curiously, the psalmist fails to provide any specific details, opting instead to mention vague generalities. The explanation for this silence about particularities may rest in the nature of the material at hand. We are dealing with a lament, even if a special kind that may be more aptly labeled a protective psalm. The speaker addresses God and refers to majestic deeds that were well known to the one who carried them out. Others who heard the prayers in the context of the synagogue would probably have filled in the missing features of the narrative.

In the shadow of these all-embracing references to wondrous deeds of God lie the related concepts of refuge and hope (vv. 1, 3, 7 for refuge, vv. 5, 6, 14 for hope). The psalmist has taken permanent refuge in God but nevertheless feels constrained to ask that this relationship continue ("Be for me a rocky refuge," v. 3a). The suppliant identifies God as his rocky crag and fortress but also his strong refuge; in the first instance the personal pronoun *you* appears in the position of predicate, whereas in the second instance it comes in the initial position signifying the subject (vv. 3 and 7). The psalmist imagines God as a remote fortress, inaccessible to enemies and safe from attack. Within the inner recesses of this refuge the suppliant finds relief from danger.

This safety in the deity brings a sense of hope even in the face of threats from active foes:

> For you are my hope, Lord;
>> Yahweh, my trust from youth.
> On you I have leaned from the womb,
>> from my mother's belly you extracted me . . .   (vv. 5-6a)

The poet's predilection toward stages of life and repeated use of temporal particles, particularly *tāmîd* (continually), demonstrates a consciousness of the significance of stability. This worshipper is "in for the long haul," come what may. Hope arises from a series of experiences that establish and confirm Yahweh's dependability, a pattern of events that becomes predictable. Hope, therefore, has nothing to do with groundless anticipation or unfounded wishes. Instead, hope consists of probable cause, for it is based on Yahweh's integrity and loving-kindness. That explains the assurance underlying the psalmist's vow "But I keep on hoping" (v. 14).

This hope pervades the suppliant's whole being, so much so that he tries to engage the entire body in expressing exhilaration over God's greatness. Mouth, lips, and tongue join in song, while the hands play on harp and lyre. The mind remembers and meditates on the reasons for such jubilation. The grateful worshipper dances to the soul's rhythm while infusing the next generation with an efficacious song.

Modern interpreters' suspicion that the author of this psalm belonged to the ranks of professional singers may mistake rhetorical flourish for literal language, but they have certainly sensed the exuberance of the psalmist. Nothing, however, absolutely precludes the assigning of the psalm to a member of a musical guild.

The use of the word "to meditate" in verse 24 recalls the first psalm and raises the expectation that language about the torah will follow. That does not happen here. Earlier when the psalmist refers to divine instruction he does not add "in the law." Instead, the teaching seems to relate to what scholars have often called saving deeds. In both places, therefore, where the poet could easily have introduced the concept of torah, he does not do so. This observation becomes especially important in assessing recent claims about intentional shaping of the Psalter in the direction of torah and wisdom. It can be argued, however, that because "righteousness" is one of the eight or nine synonyms for torah in Psalm 119, its use as the object of the verb "to meditate" in verse 24 orients the psalm toward the law. Such an argument does not seem to carry conviction, given the general tenor of the many words for God's deeds in Psalm 71.

Because the poet seems always keenly aware of danger from individuals pursuing him, he places considerable emphasis on the need for rescue. This theme punctuates the psalm from the beginning.

> By your righteous deeds deliver me and rescue me;
>   bend your ear to me and save me.   (v. 2)

> God, be not distant from me;
>   my God, rush to my aid.   (v. 12)

> . . . you will renew me once more;
>   and from the depths of the earth you will lift me again.
>   (v. 20bc)

> My lips will sing, indeed I will sing about you,
>   I myself, whom you redeemed.   (v. 23)

The formulaic expressions make it difficult to determine whether or not the danger is real or imagined. Lienhard Delekat's suggestion that many laments represent real situations of flight from avengers to the refuge of a sanctuary depends on a literal reading of the language.[1] Psalm 71 certainly lends itself to such an interpretation, although the preponderance of familiar expressions has the appearance of stereotypical discourse. The verbs in the first half of verse 2, *deliver* and *rescue*, belong to the realm of military conflict, but not exclusively so. They are often found in contexts of danger from other sources, particularly wild animals. The verb translated *redeemed* comes from the institution of slavery, whether as a result of debt or warfare, and refers to a monetary payment that frees an indentured person.

Other features of the petition for immediate action on God's part represent a spiritualizing tendency that corresponds to the concern for proper meditation. Thus the psalmist urges God to bend an ear lest his plea go unheard and contemplates inner renewal. Moreover, when he resolves to extol God's wonders through song and music, the poet varies the subjects of the verb for singing, progressing from a specific part of the body, the lips, to the whole self *(nepeš)*. Frequently, as here, this word takes the place of the pronoun I.

Perhaps the strongest indication of stereotypical language occurs in verse 20, where the poet likens the danger from which he has fled to perils in Sheol. Trapped in the turbulent waters of the depths, the psalmist prays to be extracted from the jaws of death. The verb indicates an upward journey, for Sheol was believed to comprise underground waters. Anyone who has succumbed to the raging waters of the deep desperately needs to be renewed. The poet strongly believes that God has authority over the regions of Sheol even if Death reigns there.

To what divine quality does the poet appeal when seeking help? The answer may be found in the frequency with which the word righteousness appears (vv. 2, 15, 16, 19, and 24). The poet explores the fundamental problem of justice toward and among human beings. The assumption in verse 2, that righteous dealings matter to God and characterize divine conduct, implies that God applies that characteristic as a means of rectifying things among mortals. The psalmist believes that divine righteousness towers over earthlings, reaching into the heavens. Consequently, he determines to celebrate this reality in word and song, so that others may know its magnitude. Furthermore,

---

1. Lienhard Delekat, *Asylie und Schutzorakel am Zionheiligtum* (Leiden: Brill, 1967).

he plans to ponder its grandeur in silent meditation. The term ṣidqôt
does not necessarily demand a forensic setting, as the translation *justice*
suggests. Rather the Hebrew word often has the connotation of salvific
acts on behalf of Israel. Recitation of these memorable events eventually became a fixed part of liturgy. The psalmist probably knows this
practice and vows to continue it as a means of showing gratitude for
having been lifted from the depths.

Debates over divine justice raged in the ancient world, as in modern
society. The author of Psalm 71 falls into the group of those who take
evil seriously but do not think it will have the last word. The threat of
injustice encourages loyal worshippers to rely wholly on God's help.
The poet's use of the Isaianic epithet, Holy One of Israel, reminds God
of a covenantal relationship, a bond that unites people and deity and
forms the basis for expectations on both sides (v. 22; cf. 78:41). The
psalmist's delayed use of the epithet shows that he recognizes divine
freedom even within a covenantal relationship. When praying for help,
he appeals to God's character; only when singing the divine praises
does the poet introduce the notion of covenant. For him, covenant
meant cause for gratitude, not special privilege.

A lone verb in the second half of verse 21 can easily be missed because of the repeated move from petition to trust:

You will increase my honor, embrace me, and comfort me.

The exact meaning of the verb that precedes *comfort* is uncertain. It may
connote the image of surrounding, as in an embrace, which fits nicely
with what follows. Alternatively, it may suggest a complete change, a
turning around. In any event, the poet's discomfiture has been frequently obscured by his pronounced trust, but here we can see that the
element of danger has never entirely disappeared. The time for comfort
has arrived, and its source is divine.

The poet feels his own sense of inadequacy when it comes to singing God's praises: "although I do not comprehend their number"
(v. 15b). The translators behind the versions misunderstood the last
word and construed it as writings; more probably it refers to the act of
recounting aloud God's saving works. Their magnitude renders the
psalmist speechless in the same way others who tried to describe divine
grace admit in the end that they have merely reached the beginning,

have touched only the hem of the garment. Human comprehension comes up against sublime mystery not because of deficient intellectual capacity but because God cannot be known, either in the wonders celebrated in song or in the several self-manifestations such as face, name, glory, and presence.

Despite the author's disclaimer, he succeeds admirably in communicating an intensity of feeling. The psalm freely adapts the structure of lament, moving back and forth from petition to trust. Perhaps this feature can be attributed to its character as a collage or filigree. Interpreters have pointed to the strong affinities between Psalm 71 and several others, especially the Twenty-second Psalm. This kinship with Psalm 22, which the authors of the passion narrative used freely, led to the use of Psalm 71 as the lectionary psalm for Tuesday of Holy Week. The similarities with other psalms can be seen from the following list.

Psalm 71	Other Psalms
1–3	31:2-4a
5–6, 17	22:11-12
12a	22:2, 12, 20
12b	38:13; 40:14
13	35:4, 26
18	22:31-32
19	36:7

The absence of a superscription in Psalm 71 and the prayer for speedy help from God in verse 12, which also appears in Ps 70:2, 6, have prompted some critics to connect the two psalms. This hypothesis has gained force from the fact that Psalm 70 virtually reproduces Ps 40:14-18. Some minor variations occur apart from the change of divine names from Yahweh to Elohim, the most notable being "The Lord thinks about me" in Ps 40:18 as opposed to "God, hasten to me" in Ps 70:6.

Similarities between Psalm 70 and 71 extend beyond the petition for quick help from God. Both psalms refer to "those who pursue me" by the same linguistic expression, and both stress the aspect of shame and reproach when referring to these enemies. Each psalm vocalizes an imagined speech of the foe and employs military language of deliverance. The two speeches have nothing in common, however, either grammatically or in subject matter. Both psalms use the adverb "continually" and identify the deity as "my help," but here the syntax differs greatly. Whereas the enemies in Ps 70:3 *take delight in* harming the intended victim, those in Ps 71:24 *seek* to hurt the poet. The identification of the psalmist in 70:6 (cf. 40:18) as poor and needy has no parallel in Psalm 71. However one chooses to relate these two psalms, it must be admitted that they overlap in striking ways, especially in choice of vocabulary and in the emphasis on shame.

When we stand back and try to assess the religious experience underlying Psalm 71, we are struck by the vulnerability of the remarkable poet who believed that vicious enemies stalked his every move, but also by his exceptional confidence in divine rescue. Interestingly, he seems content in the end to abide by the timetable that the deity chooses rather than closing with an appeal that the moment of deliverance not tarry (contrast Ps 70:6b, "Yahweh, do not tarry"). Thus we have returned to the beginning and to life's deepest apprehension, which so often evokes the cry, "Come, Lord." The poet who composed Psalm 71 can teach ultimate vulnerability, an openness to divine solicitude.

CHAPTER TEN

Knowing Whose You Are: Psalm 24

1 Yahweh's are the earth and all that fills it,
  the world and its inhabitants.
2 For he founded it on the seas,
  established it on the streams.
3 Who can go up to Yahweh's holy mount,
  who can stand in his sacred place?
4 The one who has innocent hands and a pure heart,
  who has not lifted up a soul to vanity,
    nor sworn to deceit.
5 That person will receive blessing from Yahweh
  and righteousness from the God of salvation.
6 This is the generation of those who seek you,
  those who seek your face, [God of] Jacob.
7 Gates, lift your heads; be lifted, eternal doors,
  so that the king of glory can enter.
8 Who is this king of glory? Yahweh, strong and mighty,
  Yahweh, valiant in battle.
9 Gates, lift your heads; be lifted, eternal doors,
  so that the king of glory can enter.
10 Who is this king of glory? Yahweh of hosts,
  he is the king of glory.

The brevity of Psalm 24 masks its profundity, for in ten short verses
the poet answers the question pertaining to ultimate ownership, clar-

ifies the qualifications for approaching sacred space, and identifies the legitimate sovereign of the universe. In doing so, she divides the poem into three distinct units (vv. 1-2, 3-6, 7-10), the last two linked by sustained use of the Hebrew verb *nāśā'* (to lift up). Underlying traditions from the myth of creation, liturgies governing admission to sacral sites, and ideology from holy war come together here in remarkable fashion to emphasize Yahweh's authority and its obligations on mortals.

Whose Are We?

The opening word in the psalm issues a resounding declaration of possession, one that functions absolutely. Nothing more needs to be said than "Yahweh's." Lest anyone miss the sweeping scope of this utterance, however, the psalmist elaborates the implications of the initial claim:

> Yahweh's are the earth and all that fills it,
>> the world and its inhabitants.   (v. 1)

In short, nothing outside the world of observable phenomena lies beyond Yahweh's domain (cf. 50:12; 89:12; 97:5). This outrageous claim takes the form of a great "nevertheless of faith," an affirmation that on the face of it seems absurd. Such absolutist claims by worshippers of gods who have demonstrated their power on the battlefield make more sense, for Israel's own deity had not fared well in conflicts involving successive peoples of Mesopotamia. One might be tempted, therefore, to consider this profession of Yahweh's worldwide sovereignty wishful thinking. We can sympathize with the desire to console oneself during hard times by maintaining the incredible, for religious people have shown extraordinary resilience over the millennia. A whole theory of cognitive dissonance has emerged as a means of explaining this phenomenon. Seldom do beliefs correspond with reality.

We should note what the poet does not say. She completely ignores the heavenly realm, an area still contested in at least one psalm that actually pushes Yahweh's claims of lordship to the limit (82). Her silence in this respect need not suggest any restricted notion of Yahweh's sovereignty, for she probably assumed that Israel's Lord ruled the heavens. Otherwise she could easily have enlarged her declaration to include the upper third of ancient cosmologies. Yahweh's dominion over Sheol, the lower third, is implicit in what the poet asserts about the stabilizing of the earth.

The unpredictability of the world has given rise to far more than the story of the flood, with its comforting promise that life can go on despite human predilection to act corruptly. Eventually, various fears regarding earth's instability fueled apocalypticism, which fused these apprehensions into a horrendous nightmare of visual imagery. None of this is evident in Psalm 24, which affirms a livable environment fully under Yahweh's control:

> For he founded it on the seas,
>   established it on the streams.   (v. 2)

The mythic conflict between God and the forces of chaos that lies behind this matter-of-fact statement seems but a remote memory. The poet depersonalizes Sea and River, choosing rather to emphasize the result of that struggle. Yahweh fixed things permanently, defeating those powers that might make life perilous and turning the human environment into a predictable habitat.

The emphatic particle *kî* (for) sets the conditions of ownership. Nothing short of an act of creation can provide a rational basis for claiming authority over the product of that unprecedented event. Because Yahweh imposed order on the earth, its occupants owe sole allegiance to him. The poet supplies the personal pronoun as subject, although the verbal form conveys that meaning in itself. The language of establishing and fixing the earth makes sense against the background of ancient belief that it rested atop pillars sunk into primordial waters. In popular sentiment tumultuous waves periodically shook these columns and produced earthquakes. Should anyone doubt the existence of underground waters, a moment's reflection on oases in the desert and artesian wells quickly allayed such skepticism and confirmed traditional belief.

Conditions Regulating Sacred Space

This absolute claim of divine ownership in Yahweh's name is matched by exclusive regulations for entering sacred space. If Yahweh truly owns the universe, the same can be said even more emphatically with respect to the holy mount. Mortals may actually erect an edifice on this spot and supervise the cult that promotes discourse between heaven and earth, but Yahweh ultimately decides who can stand in the divine presence. The psalmist knows that appearing before Yahweh is dangerous business, especially if one's inner attitude and outward conduct lack integrity. The prophets labored hard at getting that message across to the populace at large. Their moral fervor is matched by the demands imposed here on anyone who contemplates a journey to a sacred place.

> Who can go up to Yahweh's holy mount,
>   who can stand in his sacred place?
> The one who has innocent hands and a pure heart,
>   who has not lifted up a soul to vanity nor sworn to deceit.
> That person will receive blessing from Yahweh
>   and righteousness from the God of salvation.
> This is the generation of those who seek you,
>   those who seek your face, [God of] Jacob.   (vv. 3-6)

This remarkable unit has been viewed as an entrance liturgy specifying conditions for participating in cultic activities at Jerusalem. According to this interpretation, a priest asks the question in verse three and a prospective worshipper answers in the following verse. A satisfactory response then evokes a priestly permission to proceed, together with a prayer paving the way for admission into the holy place (vv. 5-6). The allocation of speakers can be different, for the statement about Yahweh's twofold signs of favor may also be seen as the climax of the worshipper's response, and the final verse may be directed at a human audience. The confusion of pronominal suffixes and the textual variants indicate that ancient readers had difficulty grasping the changes in point of view.

   If the purpose of such liturgies was to determine who could participate in the Yahwistic cult, this one fails miserably. Its stipulations for conduct cover matters that easily elude objective detection. How could guardians of the holy place ascertain whether or not a person possessed clean hands and a pure heart, or even had bowed down at a pagan altar? This rendering of the two references to vanity and fraud seems plausible; they are simply expressions for idolatry, an act of devotion that normally takes place in secret. Similarly, an undefiled mind, the real sense of "pure heart," could hardly be distinguished from its opposite. Only the claim to have clean hands, in the prophetic sense of moral uprightness vis-à-vis one's neighbor, could be shown by close examination to be false. It seems to follow that such a liturgy functions as a warning to the worshipper that standing before Yahweh should not be taken lightly. The question and answer act as guidelines for self-examination; the onus falls on the ones preparing for worship, not on priestly interrogators.

The lack of specificity with respect to the holy place gives this psalm wide appeal, enabling its survival after the collapse of the cult in Jerusalem. Although technical language abounds here, specifically "go up," "Yahweh's mount," "his holy place," "to seek," and "your face," the discourse readily conforms to that of worship in synagogues. The poet's failure to use Zion or Jerusalem where it would normally have occurred does not imply polemic, for she probably took it as a given that Yahweh's mount means Jerusalem.

The idea of standing in Yahweh's presence carried with it a pronounced sense of awe that has best been described by Rudolf Otto as *mysterium tremendum et fascinans,* a mystery that both repels and attracts.[1] The paradigmatic experience, Isaiah's call to the prophetic office in Isa 6:1-13, brings a sense of dread owing to his sinful condition and a desire to give himself wholly despite the real danger. The suffering Job notes that he will obtain personal vindication if he can enter God's presence, for he is convinced that a sinner cannot do so (Job 13:16). The author of Psalm 24 subscribes to this belief that access to holy space is restricted. She penetrates to the very heart of the issue: inner disposition and moral rectitude, along with sole allegiance spiritually.

Unbroken parallelism in this psalm opens up a different way of understanding the reference to clean hands and a pure heart. It may state differently exactly what the sequel says: clean hands have never touched

---

1. Rudolf Otto, *The Idea of the Holy* (New York: Oxford, 1958).

an idol, and pure hearts have not betrayed Yahweh by paying allegiance to other gods. The only other use of the phrase "pure hearts" (73:1) seems to suggest a right attitude toward God with respect to the apparent prosperity of the wicked. This interpretation of verse 4 requires one to ignore the Masoretic division of the verse and results in an unusually long second colon, so the earlier way of viewing the text may be preferable.

The words describing Yahweh's gift to those who attain this high moral and religious ground point to a virtual cornucopia of goodies. The mere evocation of Yahweh's blessing conjures up memories of sacred story and ritual texts featuring various kinds of blessing. In times past these gifts took the form of progeny, land, and reputation. The other word, righteousness, embraces the broad concept of justice. It designates divine faithfulness, fidelity to promise, just dealings, and deeds of salvation. Together the two concepts assure worshippers of Yahweh's favor, precisely what they have looked for when seeking the divine face. Lest it go unobserved, we should note that the poet does not promise a beatific vision. She knows full well the great care with which others protect the divine mystery, and she continues their reticence. We may seek the divine face, she suggests, but we shall, like Moses, catch only a fleeting glimpse of the holy as manifest in blessing and righteousness. That is all, but it is much.

This explication of conditions for entry into sacred space has fewer provisions than the eleven or twelve envisioned in a related psalm:

> Yahweh, who can dwell in your tent,
>   who can abide on your holy mountain?
> Those who walk in integrity
>   and do what is right,
>   who speak truth in their hearts,
>   do not slander
>   nor harm a neighbor,
>   nor lift up reproach against a companion;
> who despise those who are shameful in Yahweh's sight,
>   but honor those who revere the Lord;
> who swear to their disadvantage without retracting it;
> who do not lend money at interest,
>   nor accept a bribe against the innocent.
> Whoever does these things will not be moved.   (15:1-5)

The combination of participles and finite verbs in this liturgy emphasizes the ongoing nature of the concrete actions specified. The initial question employs a verb indicating alien status ("to sojourn"), as if acknowledging that worshippers have no claim over sacred space but depend on the favor of its owner. Like resident aliens within Israel's borders, worshippers tread safely on holy ground only if bidden to do so.

The language accentuates the ancient notion of hospitality in two ways, first by the noun "tent" but also by the verb translated "abide," which refers to pitching a tent. The later rabbinic word for divine presence, the Shekinah, also takes advantage of the rich imagery of pitching a tent somewhere. The delicate task of maintaining divine mystery while speaking of immanence gave rise to dual concepts that found expression in the ancient tent of meeting and the ark. The former preserved transcendence inasmuch as God chose when to appear in the tent, while the latter stressed Yahweh's abiding presence enthroned on the ark. Even that divine manifestation did not completely sacrifice the mystery, for Yahweh was thought to have been invisible even while sitting on the ark.

The language of hospitality has resulted in an extraordinary thought, one more appropriate to the priesthood than to ordinary laity. The worshipper is offered the prospect of residence in the sacred place, not just paying it a temporary visit. Such a daring thought would hardly have occurred to a priestly author, who would naturally have recognized the danger of introducing impurity where wrath might break out with devastating force. Ezekiel's vision of a restored Jerusalem guards against this danger by locating those deemed more holy near the temple and distancing ordinary people far enough away to preserve them from danger. The extraordinary thing about Psalm 15 is the democratizing of the idea of residence on the holy mountain. A priestly prerogative becomes the right of everyone who mirrors the divine character. Precisely what this means will now be spelled out as the answer to the question, "Yahweh, who can dwell in your tent . . . ?"

In a sense this response resembles the Decalogue, with its two tablets that cover the vertical and the horizontal dimensions of reality. Just as the Decalogue sums up the fundamentals pertaining to proper worship of Yahweh, this liturgy aims at comprehensiveness — with one decisive difference. For the Ten Commandments, the priority rests on Israel's relationship with Yahweh, and the injunction to honor parents marks a transition to the horizontal dimension. The psalm concentrates on interactions with fellow Israelites. It should not be forgotten, however, that these modes of behavior qualify individuals to enter the vertical relationship. The aim is to spend time in the divine presence.

The conditions governing entrance into sacred space combine positive and negative aspects of conduct. They also refer to concrete acts and to general attitudes. At least two words, *ṣedeq* and *'emet*, double as expressions for Yahweh's character as righteous and true. The idea underlying "speaks the truth in his heart" is not easily rendered into English. The expression conveys the notion of unity between thought and speech, an absence of dissemblance. One who speaks in accord with inner thoughts avoids the sin of hypocrisy.

The participle that begins verse 2 marks the activity as durative; those individuals who always behave with integrity eventually shape their character into that which resembles Job's, whom Yahweh singled out as a person of integrity. The word refers to wholeness, a sense of unity in which mind and body join together to produce a dependable person. The walking is accompanied by action of an appropriate kind for one who has integrity; here, too, a participle signals continuing deeds of straightforward conduct, acts flowing from righteousness. The individual is a doer of right deeds, but also a speaker of the truth. Three participles thus point to sustained or habitual integrity, just dealings, and authenticity. They also include walking, doing, and speaking, hence the totality of word, thought, and deed.

The next verse shifts to negative behavior and offers three examples. Those who hope to reside in Yahweh's presence must avoid three specifics: they must not "tread on their tongues," inflict injury on neighbors, or bring shame on acquaintances. The last two offenses are reasonably straightforward, but the first one presents a problem because of the peculiar verb. The offense seems more serious than discomfort resulting from a gadabout.

What does it mean to tread on the tongue? I have taken it to suggest scandal rather than tripping over one's speech, which inflicts self-harm. The offense must surely affect others in an adverse manner; the most likely meaning is slander, which involves a malicious use of the tongue. Speech that hurts others was particularly distressing in close-knit societies like Israel, as the frequent attempts to guard against slander suggest. The wording of the reference to reproach is sufficiently ambiguous to suggest that persons must avoid having reproach aimed at them because of the way they have treated others.

In some ways these negatively stated examples continue the earlier generalities. True, they indicate specific actions, but they mask them in the language of abstraction. Thus we read that one must not inflict evil or cause reproach. The exact kind of unpleasantry or malice remains a secret, as does the nature of the reproach. Such generality belongs to the genre itself. Instructions patterned after entrance liturgies function best when they avoid too much specificity.

The conduct alluded to in verse 4 continues verb forms, although stated in the passive initially. The importance of choosing virtuous companions has been given a theological rationale. To dwell on the sacred mountain requires one to spurn those whom Yahweh dishonors and to exalt the devout. The expression "in his eyes" occurs frequently with reference to willful behavior. People who do what appears right in their own eyes comprise a type of sinner who brings destructive consequences on oneself and others. That familiar expression applied to deity reeks with irony.

The second half of this verse may refer to a single act that has two aspects: swearing and persisting. At issue seems to be the person's reliability, a willingness to abide by a solemn promise despite the cost. Presumably, the individual in question takes an oath in ignorance of the implications of that promise but, having learned the price, continues to stand by the earlier word. This kind of dependability was essential if an oath were to survive in the judicial process. Perhaps this kind of situation occurred often, which could explain the strong resistance to oaths in the book of Ecclesiastes.

The final two acts that are introduced in verse 5 could hardly be more specific. Both of them cover the broad area of greed. They refer to charging a fee for lending money and to accepting a bribe and thus contributing to a corrupt judicial system. Usury was proscribed in Israel whenever the borrower belonged to the Israelite community, although it was permissible to charge interest to foreigners. Accepting money under the table was an absolute no-no. The word "innocent" stands out here, for Yahweh championed the cause of powerless victims who had not transgressed the law. Bribery thus went against divine preference and human decency.

A participle returns momentarily to indicate habitual practice:

"Whoever *does* these things will not be moved," although a verb has the final word. The background for the imagery belongs to the myth of creation. Just as Yahweh has sunk the pillars of the earth firmly and thus established order that will withstand every assault by the agents of chaos, the deity has formed a moral environment that secures those individuals who mirror the divine qualities here singled out for emulation. A psalm that begins with Yahweh concludes with an adverb that eventually comes to mean eternity.

These two psalms are not alone in seeking to monitor access to sacred space. According to 2 Chron 23:19, Jehoiada stationed gatekeepers to make certain that no unclean person gained entry into the temple. Nor are the psalms without parallel in stating conditions for coming before Yahweh. Deuteronomy 23:1-9 specifies those who may join the congregation of the Lord. The contrast with two prophetic texts of this type could hardly be sharper. Whereas the author of Deuteronomy focuses on instances of ritual impurity or ethnic membership, the prophetic texts are concerned with ethical behavior and proper reverence (Isa 33:13-16; Mic 6:6-8).

The question in Isa 33:14, "Who among us can dwell with a consuming fire; who among us can dwell with perpetual flames?" resembles that in Ps 15:1. The response begins the same way in both instances, specifically with the participle for walking. The prophetic text has *righteousness* rather than *integrity* but goes on to mention bribery and other acts of greed and infamy.

> Whoever walks in righteousness,
>   speaks uprightly,
>   rejects profit from oppression,
>   waves a bribe away rather than clutching it,
>   stops up ears from hearing about bloodshed,
>   shuts eyes from seeing evil —
> this one will dwell on high
>   with a fortress of rocks as refuge,
>   food provided,
>   drink assured.   (Isa 33:15-16)

The other prophetic text ponders the fundamental question: "What does God ask of mortals?" After rejecting various options, specifically burnt offerings, oil, and yes the unspeakable, sacrificing one's firstborn, Micah acknowledges that the answer has already been made known:

He has told you, mortal, what is good,
    what Yahweh seeks from you:
    only to do justice,
    love kindness,
    and to walk humbly with your God.   (Mic 6:8)

Just as Yahweh's reputation was founded on acts of justice and tender mercies, so the ones who wish to appear before the Lord must embody precisely these attributes. The word "love" carries special force, indicating that such acts arise from desire and not from constraint. We can imagine the struggle within ancient Israel over whether or not to preserve earlier practices such as human sacrifice and the temple ritual of daily sacrifices in the face of heightened ethical sensitivity. Micah, for one, casts his lot with those who opted for justice, kindness, and a humble walk before God.

These so-called entrance liturgies became occasions for summing up ethical norms for acceptance in the religious community where numerous laws existed. We note a tendency to narrow the requirements insofar as possible, a point made in later rabbinic literature by quoting various biblical injunctions, beginning with multiple demands and ending with the simple imperative in the book of Amos: "Seek me and live." Anyone who lives by that rule will never be shaken. The instructions in Psalms 15 and 24 move in this direction but devote more attention to social obligations than to specifically religious actions. In this respect we can detect an attitude akin to prophetic proclamation by Amos, Isaiah, and Micah.

Returning to Psalm 24, we have yet to consider the third part of this remarkable poem. Although separated from the previous two sections by the Hebrew *selāh,* which seems to indicate a break or pause, the third unit is linked with what immediately precedes it by the verb "to lift up." This verb occurs four times in verses 7 and 9, each time in its literal sense with reference to raising gates. Scholars have sought to understand this curious liturgy against the background of the narrative about the bringing of the ark to Jerusalem, although this sacred palladium is not mentioned.

Gates, lift your heads,
  be lifted, eternal doors,
  so that the king of glory can enter.
Who is this king of glory?
  Yahweh, strong and mighty,
  Yahweh, valiant in battle.
Gates, lift your heads,
  be lifted, eternal doors,
  so that the king of glory can enter.
Who is this king of glory?
  Yahweh of hosts,
  he is the king of glory.   (Ps 24:7-10)

The combination of imperatives and questions gives the impression of differing perspectives. Those on the outside request admission from persons within, who dare not open the gates until they discover the identity of the one seeking entry. The third section of the psalm thus provides a graphic example of someone wanting to dwell in sacred space and being asked for credentials. In this instance, however, the one seeking admission is Yahweh, whose credentials are beyond question.

The language of this liturgy abounds in martial imagery, particularly the divine epithet "Yahweh of hosts" and the unusual expression "king of glory." The precise meaning of hosts cannot be determined, for it refers both to human militia and to supernatural forces. In the book of Exodus Yahweh is identified as a warrior (15:3) and healer (15:26), the latter as if to temper any excessive emphasis on the deity's bellicosity. The liturgy involving the king of glory has no such softening of the martial language.

A moment's reflection on the language of this ritual suggests that it aims to identify the true sovereign of the city as the one who wishes to take up residence there. This claim may represent a response by the postexilic community to Ezekiel's report that Yahweh abandoned Jerusalem and dwelt in Babylonia. Whereas this prophet's vision of a restored holy city concludes with a mighty shout, "Yahweh is there" (Ezek 48:35), which echoes the old epithet "Yahweh is his name," the psalmist insists that the king of glory has returned to Jerusalem and awaits the lifting of gates. Just as the glory once departed, it now returns. The unusual expression "the king of glory" may have been chosen to link these two texts in popular imagination.

The bold poetic language imagines the impossible, the raising of heavy gates like garage doors. Inanimate stone is addressed like a person; those seeking entry ask it to ascend so as no longer to present an obstacle. The dramatic effect comes at the expense of obscuring Yahweh's ability to negotiate any obstacle, however formidable. The poet's primary interest falls on Yahweh's identity as king of glory, not on obliging gates and doors.

Conclusion

The time has come to take another look at this journey through the book of Psalms and along the byways formed by numerous interpreters seeking to plumb the depths of its riches. We have paused long enough to examine the major features of the several collections, particularly those attributed to David, Asaph, Korah's descendants, but also to individuals such as Moses, Solomon, and Ethan, and discrete units, for example, the Songs of Ascents and the Hallelujah Psalms. We have compared these biblical psalms to similar texts in the Bible outside the book of Psalms and to related deutero-canonical and noncanonical literature. This exploration has enabled us to appreciate the scope of the psalmic texts from the two standpoints of religious teachings and literary artistry.

The aim of Part II was to illustrate various modes of interpreting the Psalms. The earliest approach to them emphasized the human origin of this literature as opposed to revelation from above. The psalms represent prayers to the Lord, either in praise or in petition. A vexing feature of these prayers, the cursing of enemies, elicited some small effort to understand how ancient worshippers could shift from intense ardor before the deity to violent expressions of hatred for enemies. The study of Psalms as a resource for the historical reconstruction of Israelite existence was examined, with special attention paid to iconography in the ancient Near East. A third approach, the classification of Psalms on the basis of types and the search for social settings for individual psalms, especially in the cult, was treated in some detail. Recent forays into artistic design and theological editing of the Psalter are held up for scrutiny and critique. An excursus questioning the existence of wisdom psalms rounds out this analysis of approaches to the book of Psalms.

The third part allows readers to zero in on four psalms of quite different complexion and to see how one interpreter engages the text. These particular psalms tackle the perennial problem of theodicy, endeavor to determine the essence of authentic worship, explore the increasingly distressing problem of aging, and evaluate the conditions for entering sacred space and confronting the holy. I recognize that these attempts to appreciate the literary artistry and theological sensitivity of the ancient poets responsible for these psalms has only touched the hem of the garment, but if my small effort encourages readers to study the book of Psalms for themselves with fresh eyes, I shall consider the result worth the bother of writing this book.

Select Bibliography

Allen, Leslie C. *Psalms 101–150*. WBC. Waco: Word, 1983.

Anderson, Bernhard W. *Out of the Depths*. Philadelphia: Westminster, 1983.

Barth, Christoph. *Introduction to the Psalms*. New York: Scribners, 1966.

Bellinger, W. H. *Psalms: Reading and Studying the Book of Praises*. Peabody: Hendrickson, 1990.

Brueggemann, Walter. *Abiding Astonishment: Psalms, Modernity, and the Making of History*. Louisville: Westminster/John Knox, 1991.

———. *The Message of the Psalms: A Theological Commentary*. Minneapolis: Augsburg, 1984.

Craigie, Peter C. *Psalms 1–50*. Waco: Word, 1983.

Dahood, Mitchell. *Psalms*. 3 vols. Garden City, N.Y.: Doubleday, 1965, 1968, 1970.

Gerstenberger, Erhard S. *Psalms: Part I, with an Introduction to Cultic Poetry*. FOTL 14. Grand Rapids: Eerdmans, 1988.

Gunkel, Hermann. *An Introduction to the Psalms*. Macon, Ga.: Mercer University Press, 1998.

———. *The Psalms: A Form-Critical Introduction*. Philadelphia: Fortress, 1967.

Holladay, William L. *The Psalms through Three Thousand Years: Prayerbook of a Cloud of Witnesses*. Minneapolis: Fortress, 1993.

Hopkins, Denise Dombkowski. "Psalms 15 and 24: The Moral Individual in the Religious Life of Early Israel." Ph.D. diss., Vanderbilt University, 1985.

Kraus, Hans-Joachim. *Psalms 60–150*. Minneapolis: Augsburg, 1989.

———. *Psalms 1–59*. Minneapolis: Augsburg, 1988.

————. *Theology of the Psalms*. Minneapolis: Augsburg, 1986.

Limburg, James. "Psalms, Book of." In *Anchor Bible Dictionary*, vol. V, pp. 522-36. New York: Doubleday, 1992.

Mays, James L. *Psalms*. Louisville: John Knox, 1994.

McCann, J. Clinton, Jr. "Psalms." In *NIB*, vol. IV, pp. 641-1280. Nashville: Abingdon, 1996.

Miller, Patrick D. *They Cried to the Lord: The Form and Theology of Biblical Prayer*. Minneapolis: Fortress, 1994.

————. *Interpreting the Psalms*. Philadelphia: Fortress, 1986.

Mowinckel, Sigmund. *The Psalms in Israel's Worship*. Nashville: Abingdon, 1962.

Simon, Uriel. *Four Approaches to the Book of Psalms*. Albany, N.Y.: SUNY, 1991.

Stuhlmueller, Carroll. "Psalms." In *Harper's Bible Commentary*, pp. 433-94. San Francisco: Harper and Row, 1988.

Tate, Marvin E. *Psalms 51–100*. WBC. Waco: Word, 1990.

Vossberg, Lothar. *Studien zum Reden vom Schöpfer in den Psalmen*. Munich: Kaiser, 1975.

Weiser, Artur. *The Psalms*. Philadelphia: Westminster, 1962.

Westermann, Claus. *Praise and Lament in the Psalms*. Atlanta: John Knox, 1981.

————. *The Psalms: Structure, Content, and Message*. Minneapolis: Fortress, 1980.

Whybray, Norman. *Reading the Psalms as a Book*. JSOTSS 222. Sheffield: Sheffield Academic Press, 1996.

Wieder, Laurance. *The Poet's Book of Psalms*. New York and Oxford: Oxford University Press, 1995.

Wilson, Gerald H. *The Editing of the Hebrew Psalter*. SBLDS 76. Chico, Calif.: Scholars Press, 1985.

Zenger, Erich. *A God of Vengeance? Understanding the Psalms of Divine Wrath*. Louisville: Westminster/John Knox, 1995.

Glossary

Ab   Roughly the month of July

Eighteen Benedictions   The earliest statement of Jewish praise or prayer, now nineteen in number. Another name for these benedictions is Amidah.

Hallel   Praise (from the Hebrew verb *hālal,* to praise

Masoretic Text   The Hebrew Bible (Old Testament) as preserved by Jewish scribes who were known as Masoretes, or pointers (referring to the system of vocalization they developed for the consonantal text)

Mishnah   A collection of oral interpretation of Jewish traditional learning dating to c. 200 CE.

Septuagint   A translation of the Hebrew Bible into Greek, often written as LXX

Ta'anith   A tractate of the Mishnah

Talmud   Ancient rabbinic writings consisting of the Mishnah and the discussions relating to it, designated Gemara

Index of Subjects

Index of Authors

175

Index of Biblical References

Joel
2:12-14 — 44
2:28-29 [3:1-2] — 138
4:6-8 [3:6-8] — 28
4:18 [3:18] — 30

Amos
2:6-8 — 28
3:2 — 35
3:15 — 27
5:14 — 58
5:15 — 44
6:5 — 5
9:2-4 — 64

Jonah
2:2-9 — 42

Micah
6:6-8 — 164
6:8 — 165

Habakkuk
3:1-19 — 42
3:3 — 5
3:9 — 5
3:13 — 5
3:19 — 5

Zechariah
11:4-17 — 61
14:8 — 30

Malachi
3:16 — 31

Mark
14:26 — 3

Luke
1:46b-55 — 51

John
1:1-3 — 51

Acts
4:24 — 3

1 Corinthians
14:26 — 3

Ephesians
5:19 — 3

Philippians
2:6-11 — 51

Colossians
1:15-20 — 51

Hebrews
5-7 — 74

Revelation
21:9-27 — 44
22:1-2 — 30

Tobit
3:2-6 — 44
3:11b-15 — 44
3:15b-17 — 44
8:5b-7 — 44
13:1-17 — 44

Judith
16:1-17 — 44

Wisdom of Solomon
7:1-6 — 65
16:24–19:22 — 45

Sirach
3:23 — 46
24:9 — 51
29:21 — 45
36:1-22 — 46
39:16-31 — 45
41:17–42:8 — 146
43 — 77
43:24-25 — 77
50:25-26 — 94
51:1-11 — 45
51:13-30 — 2

1 Esdras
4:13-40 — 59
4:34-40 — 59

Psalms of Solomon — 88

Index of Hebrew and Greek Words

GREEK WORDS